D0662517

TIMBER PRESS
POCKET GUIDE TO
Water Garden Plants

TIMBER PRESS
POCKET GUIDE TO

Water Garden Plants

GREG SPEICHERT
and
SUSAN SPEICHERT

TIMBER PRESS
PORTLAND • LONDON

Frontispiece: *Oenanthe javanica* 'Flamingo' meanders over rocks beside a waterfall, while *Cyperus alternifolius* 'Nanus' thrives in the pond at the right.

Mention of trademark, proprietary product, or vendor does not constitute a guarantee or warranty of the product by the publisher or authors and does not imply its approval to the exclusion of other products or vendors.

Copyright © 2008 by Greg Speichert and Sue Speichert. All rights reserved.

Published in 2008 by
Timber Press, Inc.

The Haseltine Building
133 S.W. Second Avenue, Suite 450
Portland, Oregon 97204-3527
www.timberpress.com

2 The Quadrant
135 Salusbury Road
London NW6 6RJ
www.timberpress.co.uk

Designed by Christi Payne
Printed in China

ISBN-13: 978-0-88192-846-4

Library of Congress Cataloging-in-Publication Data

Speichert, C. Greg.
    Timber Press pocket guide to water garden plants / Greg Speichert and
Sue Speichert. -- 1st ed.
        p. cm.
    Includes bibliographical references and index.
    ISBN-13: 978-0-88192-846-4
    1. Aquatic plants--Handbooks, manuals, etc. 2. Water gardens--Handbooks,
manuals, etc. I. Speichert, Sue. II. Title. III. Title: Pocket guide to water garden plants.
    SB423.S627 2008
    635.9'674--dc22
                                                        2008008878

A catalog record for this book is also available from the British Library.

Acknowledgments

Thank you to the staff at Timber Press for making this pocket guide and the larger reference on which it is based, *Encyclopedia of Water Garden Plants*, available to the gardening public.

About This Book

This guide provides practical information on the selection, siting, planting, and aftercare of a full range of plants for ponds and wet soils. It opens with plant suggestions for specific purposes and locations, so that anyone wanting help to find an appropriate choice for a particular landscape setting may do so quickly, without having to wade through pages of descriptions.

The main portion of the book consists of plant descriptions organized into sections and arranged in alphabetical order by scientific name. The brief descriptions indicate the likely mature size of a plant grown under normal garden conditions and care. The eventual height and spread of a specific plant, however, will vary according to the conditions in which it is grown—temperature, moisture, fertility, exposure, soil pH, competition, care, pruning, and so forth.

Measurements for the pond sizes suggested in this book are as follows:

Tub and container water gardens	3 feet (90 cm) or less across
Small pond	4–6 feet (1.2–1.8 m) across
Medium pond	7–9 feet (2.1–2.7 m) across
Large pond	10 feet (3 m) or more across

The book concludes with two maps showing USDA hardiness zones for North America and Europe, a list of retail suppliers who carry a good range of water garden plants, and a short list of recommended books for further information.

CONTENTS

Opposite: A tub garden displays a dwarf hardy waterlily with *Peltandra virginica* on the right and *Equisetum hyemale* on the left.

PREFACE

Water gardening is the fastest-growing gardening pasttime in North America. Contributing to this rapid growth are two groups of homeowners: those who are discovering what the Japanese have known for hundreds of years—the satisfaction of creating a water feature in their own backyard—and those with a wet area on their property that can't be planted with the usual garden plant.

Unlike most books on water gardening which concentrate on designing and constructing a water garden, this handy volume focuses on the plants that thrive in water and wet soils. Starting with hardy and tropical waterlilies and lotus, the book moves beyond these traditional water garden inhabitants to include the full range of aquatic plants: marginals that grow with their roots in the wet soil but with most of their foliage above water, floaters, bog plants, water irises, and submerged plants. The choices are numerous, and whether you are new to water gardening or experienced, looking for a single plant to fill a small container or for a group of plants to create a larger water feature, this book can help you find and successfully grow the best plants for your landscape.

Opposite: The large, round leaves of a pink-flowered lotus contrast with the narrow, pendant leaves of a variegated grass to add interest to a waterfall planting.

INTRODUCTION

In most ways, water plants are like any other kind of plant. They have roots, leaves, stems, and usually flowers. They need sunlight and food to grow, air to breathe, and water to drink. What makes water plants, or aquatics, different is their ability to grow in a wet, watery environment. Some require only a few inches of water, others a few feet, and still others tolerate only wet or moist soil.

This guide divides water garden plants into groups of plants with similar cultivation requirements. **Waterlilies**, the plants most often associated with a pond, grow in the middle of the pond with their roots and stems below water and their round leaves on the water surface. Their many-petaled flowers vary from round to star-shaped; some float on the water and others are held on stems several inches out of the water. Their color

and fragrance also vary widely. Hardy waterlilies survive winters in colder climates, while tropical waterlilies cannot withstand a winter freeze and need special care during colder months. The best way to tell whether a waterlily is hardy or tropical is to look at the edges of the leaves: hardy waterlily leaves are smooth at their edges, tropical waterlily leaves are highly toothed.

Lotus are similar to waterlilies but hold their leaves and flowers well above the water. The bowl-shaped, highly fragrant flowers are delicately colored; pink and white are common flower colors, but yellow and a dark pink that is almost red are also available. The very round leaves of lotus stand out of the water like inverted parasols and are covered with a velvety wax that makes raindrops roll around like little balls of mercury. The plants grow from 6 inches

Hardy waterlilies fill a planter in a shady pond to help them bloom more. Marginals growing along the back edge of the pond, left to right, are *Cyperus alternifolius*, *Carex elata* 'Knightshayes', *Saururus cernuus*, *Carex muskingumensis*, and *Myriophyllum aquaticum*.

Opposite: An abundant stand of blue-flowered *Pontederia cordata* (center) is surrounded by white-flowered *Saururus cernuus*, with black-stemmed *Colocasia esculenta* 'Violet Stem' and *Cyperus longus* in the back of the pond, variegated *Canna* 'Pretoria' and a Louisiana iris on the right, and *Lysimachia nummularia* 'Aurea' creeping over rocks in the foreground.

(15 cm) to 6 feet (1.8 m) tall. Smaller selections, called bowl lotus, thrive in containers that are less than one foot (30 cm) wide and in just a few inches of soil and water. Lotus also grow well in bogs with a few inches of standing water.

Marginal water plants grow at the edge of the pond with their roots in the soil but with most of their foliage above the soil and out of the water. They are also referred to as emergent because their leaves emerge above the soil and water. Some marginals grow in soil that is only moist or wet, while others prefer soil that is a few inches under water. The plants can be more than 6 feet (1.8 m) or less than 2 inches (5 cm) tall. Some are clump forming and stay where they are put. Others are rambling and come up all over the pond edge.

Among the many irises known to horticulture is a very useful group that grows in water. Some of them grow best in shallow water, while others only tolerate wet soil for part of the year. Flower colors vary widely, and foliage may be all green or variegated. All are easy to grow.

Plants that are not waterlilies but that do grow in soil several inches below the water surface and hold their leaves and flowers on top of the water are grouped together as waterlily-like plants. All make excellent contributions to container water gardens as well as in-ground ponds.

Floating water plants sit on the water surface with no need of pot or soil. They are extremely easy to grow. All they need is a container that holds water. Their roots dangle down in the water, drawing nutrients that could otherwise cause an algae bloom. Among the least expensive of all water plants, they are usually bought fresh each year by most water gardeners. In the winter, simply add them to the compost pile or use them to mulch around perennials; because of their high-nitrogen content, they add nutrients to the soil even after being removed from the pond.

Plants that grow entirely underwater are called submerged water plants. They are also known as oxygenators for their ability to add oxygen to the water. This group includes the familiar aquarium plants that are grown in children's goldfish bowls. It also encompasses the many underwater plants that provide cover and spawning ground for fish in natural lakes, rivers, and streams. Many submerged water plants have colorful foliage that glistens underwater, and several even have flowers that float on the water surface during the summer. They are very easy to grow and need very little care to make their important contribution to the ecology and life of the pond.

Cultivating Water Plants

Water plants are not fussy or particular about the container in which they are planted. They do, however, have a few basic requirements, namely, the right amount of moisture, sunlight, and food to grow and flower well. As long as these needs are met, water plants grow well, usually with little additional care or attention.

Pots

Gardeners who have rubber, concrete, or fiberglass ponds often grow their water plants in pots. Pots are also good to use in earth-bottom ponds to contain running plants and to make them look more full. The purpose of a pot is to keep plant and soil together in the pond, without dirtying the water or damaging the pond.

Open-weave and fabric baskets are used by water gardeners because they allow the water to diffuse through all the pot surfaces, enabling the plant to pull more nutrients from the water. This is especially important for plants grown for their filtration qualities. Plants growing in open-weave or fabric baskets may need transplanting more frequently, as their roots will naturally seek the open water and eventually break through a basket.

Hard-sided plastic pots may have one or more bottom holes, or none at all. Pots without holes are excellent for making into miniature patio or table-top ponds.

In large natural ponds, waterlilies are often planted without pots. Here, burlap bags with soil hold the plants in place. As the lily grows, the burlap disintegrates and the plant moves into the soil on its own.

Some submerged plants are simply placed in a bunch, weighted, and tossed to the bottom of the pond. The muck that builds on the pond's floor is often enough for the plants to root into for the growing season.

Soil

Plants generally need a potting medium for anchorage, fertilization, and moisture retention. Soil keeps plants standing up straight and prevents them from falling over. It holds the nutrients and water that the plants need to flourish. Clay garden soil is ideal for all water plants. It holds more nutrients for the plant to absorb, and it holds the plants in place.

Sandy garden soil or even pure sand is good for short plants with a mounded or creeping habit, but the plants will need to be fertilized regularly. Potting soils and other bagged garden soils usually contain a high degree of organic matter, which can be harmful, even deadly, for water plants. Bagged soil also often contains vermiculite and perlite, which float to the water surface once they enter the pond and are unsightly there. Pea gravel and small pebbles are ideal for filtration plants, whose roots can catch nutrients as they pass through the crevices created by the small stones.

Cat litter made from calcified clay also works well as a potting medium. Be sure the litter has

A dwarf waterlily fills a tub garden along with upright *Typha laxmannii*, floating *Eichhornia crassipes*, pendant *Juncus effusus* 'Spiralis', dark-green-leaved *Hydrocharis morsus-ranae*, and yellow-flowered *Iris pseudacorus*.

Small brown stones top off the soil, providing contrast for a waterfall planting that includes *Arundo donax* 'Variegata' at far left, black-leaved *Colocasia esculenta* 'Black Magic', and in the back, yellow-striped *Canna* 'Pretoria' and reddish-leaved *Canna* 'Phasion'. In the foreground are *Cyperus alternifolius* 'Nanus' backed by *Oenanthe sarmentosa*.

not been deodorized or treated chemically. Pure calcified clay is mined from the earth, cleaned, baked, and pulverized. It has about the same good nutrient- and moisture-retention qualities as clay soil. Although cat litter can have some dust to it when it comes out of the bag, do not rinse it off before use as it will dissolve.

Rock wool is clean and sterile and certainly less dirty looking than clay soil, sand, or pea gravel. Cocoa fiber looks like brown strands of straw that have been woven together. It is ideal for filtration plants. The material acts like pea gravel, allowing water to flow over the plants' roots. Like rock wool, cocoa fiber is lightweight and needs to be weighted down.

Whatever medium is used, it should be topped with pea gravel, sand, or stones to help prevent fish from digging the soil out of the pot and to reduce the amount of weeds that can grow in the soil. A pot of soil dressed with a topping looks prettier, turning a ho-hum "swamp weed" into a water garden knockout. Pea gravel generally is the most popular topping. Sand is the nicest to use on submerged plants and tropical lilies because it is softer and lessens the possibility of damaging the crown of the plant. Toppings should be dark colored, making the plants look greener. Light colors will make the plants look more yellow. Larger stones are generally used where large koi or goldfish live in the pond to prevent them from sucking smaller plants out of the pot. Some water gardeners have even used slabs of black slate to keep lilies in their containers.

Fertilizer

Fertilizer provides the necessary building blocks for plants to live and grow. It works by manipulating three basic ingredients: nitrogen (N), phosphorus (P), and potassium (K). Depending on the amounts of each of these ingredients, fertilizers can cause plants to grow more leaves, set more fruit, or produce more flowers.

Micronutrients also play an important role. Called trace elements because plants need them only in small amounts, they include calcium, magnesium, and sulfur, as well as iron, manganese, copper, zinc, and boron. Most plants, including water plants, require their soil and water pH to range between 6.5 and 8.5 to be able to absorb micronutrients properly.

Use a fertilizer formulated for pot plants. Organic forms of fertilizer should be used for water plants with great caution, or better yet, not at all. In the pond, organic fertilizers develop more quickly and remain in the soil longer, and can burn plants' roots, ultimately causing their death. Manure, for example, is often suggested as a fertilizer for pond plants. If it is not very, very well aged and fully composted, however, manure will continue to rot while underwater and will inhibit plants' growth and health.

Often pond owners use fertilizers for perennials, trees, or shrubs instead of fertilizer made specially for aquatics. Although these fertilizers are not likely to harm fish or other wildlife, they have been made for very different conditions and may not respond the same when placed in water.

One good rule of thumb, regardless of the type of fertilizer used, is to alternate feedings to lessen the effect of any fertilizer leaching into the pond. Fertilize half the plants one week, and then wait two weeks in spring or one week in summer before fertilizing the others. Always, always follow the manufacturer's directions when fertilizing any plants.

Pests and Diseases

Like other plants, water garden plants are susceptible to damage by animals, insects, and diseases. Among the most destructive pests of a water garden are animals. Literally overnight they can destroy a pond.

Animals

Although it is fun to see herons, geese, swans, and ducks visiting a pond, these birds love the same plants you do, but for food and nest building.

Cats generally bother water gardens for the fish buffet, and dogs are a problem only when they cannot resist playing in the water. Deer pose a browsing problem, as they do for the rest of the garden. They often enter ponds that have broad shelves and can put holes in the liner. They love waterlily flowers.

Crayfish move into a pond unbeknownst to the pond keeper and start eating away at the base of submerged plants, especially sagittarias and vallisnerias, dislodging them and usually eating the crowns. Koi give interest to a backyard pond and may never touch the plants. Then one day you find mud and coleslaw. The koi are not at fault; they are plant eaters and when you add them to a pond, you are putting plants directly in harm's way.

Voles and mice are generally not a problem until winter, when they use plants for food and cover. Muskrats love to burrow through the pond liner and build tunnels. They also love to collect plants both to build their homes and to eat, so they are doubly destructive. Nutria are giant plant-eating rodents imported from South America for the fur trade. They have escaped

White-flowered *Myosotis scorpioides* and yellow-flowered *Ranunculus flammula* intermix at the left edge of a pond in which a hardy *Nymphaea* 'Pearl of the Pool' is growing. Surrounding the pond are a variegated, narrow-leaved *Glyceria* and a solid green, heart-shaped *Pontederia* at the left, a triangular-leaved *Thalia* and upright-leaved *Cyperus longus* in the right background, and densely flowered *Baldellia ranunculoides* f. *repens* at the far right. In the foreground are bamboolike *Phragmites australis* and a tiny, whitish flowered *Alisma*.

and naturalized in some areas of North America and can devastate a pond like muskrats, but on a grander scale.

Raccoons damage plants while foraging for fish and frogs in a pond. They also seem to love chewing up water hyacinth (*Eichhornia*). They can destroy dozens of the plants in a single night, just chewing them up rather than eating them. They will tip over pots and uproot things in search of their prize.

Snails eat algae in fish tanks with plastic plants, but in ponds they also eat plants. Apple snails and Columbian ram's horn snails are voracious eaters, attacking waterlilies and other plants that are found below the water surface. Handpicking seems to be the only cure.

Fish share a backyard pond with hardy waterlily *Nymphaea* 'Sunrise'. *Cyperus alternifolius* 'Nanus' and *C. isocladus* grow in front of a Louisiana iris on the left.

Insects

Several insect pests bother water garden plants. Dragonflies are *not* among them, despite the myth that they harm plants. Dragonflies eat bugs and are great for a pond; every pond should have them.

China mark moth is the most prevalent of the water-damaging insects. It cuts little pieces of plant material to cover itself while it sleeps or feeds. The moths are generally confined to waterlilies and waterlily-like plants, but they will float off to infect other plants. Large infestations make the pond look like it is slowly being chopped into coleslaw.

Aphids, whether black, green, or yellow, are all destructive and cause a lot of damage, yellowing leaves and destroying buds and flowers. Their activity usually attracts other insects. Caddysfly larvae do little damage but in high numbers they can be annoying, constantly chewing off bits of plants to add to their protective cases. Yellow- and black-striped cucumber beetles do a great job of destroying the flowers of *Canna* and *Butomus*. Japanese beetles can damage a lot of plants in the garden, including marginal water plants. Lotus borer often shows up after lotus have been growing in the pond for a few years but rarely causes fatalities.

Mealybugs are not a problem outdoors but can become a problem indoors when plants are overwintered. Spider mites are generally not a problem except when plants are in winter storage and when they are grown in very hot, dry summers. Weevils bother waterlily leaves and hibiscus flowers. Whiteflies usually go for *Hibiscus*, *Mentha*, *Mimulus*, and *Ruellia*, but they have shown up on other plants also.

Diseases

Among the diseases affecting water plants, crown rot is the most devastating for waterlilies. It spreads when infected plants are introduced to the pond. Experts say there is no control but destruction of infected plants. Yellowing leaves in midsummer and no new growth are indicators of the disease as is the eventual rotting away of the crowns.

Fusarium is a common soil- or water-borne fungus that affects only a few aquatics. Canna rust will appear as orange dust on the leaves of cannas. Sooty mold is accompanied by an insect infestation and is the result of the insects giving off a sugary secretion called honeydew. The fungus feeds on both the honeydew and the plant. Viruses are everywhere and can affect virtually any plant. The one most often encountered in the pond is canna virus. The plants look burned and never recover. The only control is to destroy the plant and start over.

PLANTS FOR SPECIFIC PURPOSES AND LOCATIONS

The categories that follow are designed to suggest the qualities and uses of selected plants described in this volume. The lists are not comprehensive, and readers are encouraged to refer to the plant descriptions for information on a cultivar's suitability for a specific location or use.

Plants to Filter Pond Water

These plants are excellent for filtering algae out of pond water wherever they are located in the pond but are more efficient if planted where there is some water flow. Use them in a stream, waterfall, or biological filter, or in a bog designed to accommodate water plants.

Acorus calamus 'Variegatus'
Cyperus alternifolius
Eichhornia crassipes
Glyceria maxima 'Variegata'
Iris versicolor and cultivars
Iris virginica and cultivars
Juncus effusus and cultivars
Juncus inflexus 'Afro'
Ludwigia arcuta 'Grandiflora'
Ludwigia peruviana
Mentha aquatica
Oenanthe javanica 'Flamingo'
Pistia stratiotes 'Aqua Velvet'
Sagittaria latifolia
Scirpus
Typha

Plants for Patio and Table-Top Ponds

Acorus calamus 'Variegatus'
Acorus gramineus and cultivars
Alternanthera reineckii
Bacopa caroliniana
Bacopa monnieri
Baldellia ranunculoides f. *repens*
Baumea rubiginosa 'Variegata'

Carex flacca
Carex muskingumensis 'Oehme'
Ceratopteris thalictroides
Colocasia esculenta 'Black Magic'
Cotula coronopifolia
Cyperus alternifolius 'Gracilis'
Cyperus isocladus
Dichromena
Echinodorus cordifolius 'Marble Queen'
Eichhornia crassipes
Glyceria maxima 'Variegata'
Hydrocleys nymphoides
Hydrocotyle sibthorpioides 'Variegata'
Hygrophila difformis 'Variegata'
Juncus effusus cultivars
Juncus glaucus
Juncus inflexus 'Afro'
Lemna
Ludwigia peploides
Lysimachia nummularia 'Aurea'
Marsilea mutica 'Micro Mini'
Mimulus guttatus 'Variegatus'
Mimulus 'Lothian Fire'
Myosotis scorpioides cultivars
Nymphoides geminata
Nymphoides indica
Oenanthe javanica 'Flamingo'
Physostegia leptophylla
Pistia stratiotes 'Aqua Velvet'
Pontederia cordata 'Crown Point'
Pontederia cordata 'Spoon River'
Ranunculus flammula 'Thor'
Rotala rotundifolia
Ruellia brittoniana cultivars
Sagittaria 'Bloomin' Baby'
Sagittaria latifolia 'Flore Pleno'
Samolus parviflorus
Typha minima
Veronica
Wedelia trilobata

Opposite: Hardy waterlily *Nymphaea* 'Queen of Whites' brightens a partly shaded corner in a pond.

Plants that Tolerate Shade

Acorus calamus 'Variegatus'
Acorus gramineus 'Ogon'
Acorus gramineus 'Variegatus'
Acrostichum danaeifolium
Alisma plantago-aquatica
Alternanthera reineckii
Apios americana
Aponogeton distachyus
Bacopa caroliniana
Bacopa monnieri
Calla palustris
Caltha palustris
Carex flacca 'Bias'
Carex muskingumensis 'Oehme'
Ceratopteris thalictroides
Colocasia esculenta 'Black Magic'
Colocasia esculenta 'Metallica'
Colocasia jensii
Crinum americanum
Cyperus alternifolius 'Gracilis'
Dichromena colorata
Dulichium arundinaceum
Echinodorus cordifolius
Eichhornia crassipes
Elodea canadensis
Epilobium hirsutum
Equisetum fluviatile
Equisetum hyemale
Glyceria maxima 'Variegata'
Hydrocotyle sibthorpioides 'Variegata'
Hygrophila corymbosa 'Stricta'
Hygrophila difformis 'Variegata'
Hymenocallis liriosome
Iris versicolor
Iris virginica
Juncus effusus 'Gold Strike'
Juncus effusus 'Unicorn'
Juncus inflexus 'Afro'
Lemna
Lobelia siphilitica 'Alba'
Ludwigia arcuta 'Grandiflora'
Lychnis flos-cuculi
Lysimachia nummularia 'Aurea'
Lysimachia thyrsiflora
Marsilea mutica 'Micro Mini'
Mentha aquatica

Menyanthes trifoliata
Mimulus alatus 'Snow Crystal'
Mimulus ringens
Myosotis scorpioides cultivars
Nymphoides indica
Oenanthe javanica 'Flamingo'
Orontium aquaticum
Peltandra virginica
Petasites hybridus
Phyla lanceolata
Physostegia leptophylla
Pistia stratiotes
Ranunculus longirostris
Rotala rotundifolia
Ruellia brittoniana 'Chi Chi'
Sagittaria latifolia 'Flore Pleno'
Samolus parviflorus
Saururus cernuus
Sium suave
Sparganium
Veronica
Wedelia trilobata

Rooted Floaters

Arranging potted plants in the pond so that the pots don't show is sometimes tricky. We recommend using certain plants as underplantings at the base of taller plants. These smaller plants can be planted with their larger neighbor or kept in their own pots. The following plants are especially favored because their stems float on the water surface but stay rooted in their container, so they won't float around all over the pond.

Bacopa monnieri
Calla palustris
Ludwigia arcuta 'Grandiflora'
Marsilea mutica
Mentha aquatica
Menyanthes trifoliata
Phyla lanceolata

Plants for Streams and Waterfalls

Acorus gramineus and cultivars
Bacopa
Baldellia ranunculoides f. *repens*
Carex flacca 'Bias'

Carex muskingumensis 'Oehme'
Cotula coronopifolia
Echinodorus cordifolius
Eleocharis acicularis
Glyceria maxima 'Variegata'
Hydrocotyle sibthorpioides 'Variegata'
Hygrophila difformis 'Variegata'
Justicia americana
Ludwigia arcuta 'Grandiflora'
Lysimachia nummularia 'Aurea'
Marsilea mutica
Mentha aquatica
Menyanthes trifoliata
Mimulus guttatus 'Variegatus'
Myosotis scorpioides and cultivars
Oenanthe javanica 'Flamingo'
Phyla lanceolata
Ranunculus
Rotala rotundifolia
Samolus parviflorus
Veronica
Wedelia trilobata

Plants for Attracting Butterflies
Asclepias incarnata
Canna
Cotula coronopifolia
Epilobium hirsutum
Hygrophila corymbosa 'Stricta'
Hygrophila difformis 'Variegata'
Iris versicolor and cultivars
Iris virginica and cultivars
Lobelia cardinalis
Lobelia siphilitica 'Alba'
Lysimachia terrestris
Mentha aquatica
Myosotis scorpioides 'Pinkie'
Myosotis scorpioides 'Wisconsin'
Nelumbo
Nymphaea
Phyla lanceolata
Physostegia leptophylla
Pontederia cordata and cultivars
Preslia cervina
Ranunculus acris
Ruellia brittoniana
Saururus cernuus

Sium suave
Stachys palustris
Veronica americana

Pink Lotus
Nelumbo 'Carolina Queen'
Nelumbo 'Charles Thomas'
Nelumbo 'Double Pink'
Nelumbo 'Momo Botan'
Nelumbo 'Pekinensis Rubra'
Nelumbo 'Perry's Super Star'

White Lotus
Nelumbo 'Alba Plena'
Nelumbo 'Chawan Basu'
Nelumbo 'Chong Shui Hua'
Nelumbo 'Debbie Gibson'
Nelumbo 'Shirokunshi'
Nelumbo 'Xiamen Bowl'

Day-blooming Tropical Waterlilies
Nymphaea 'Blue Beauty' (blue)
Nymphaea 'Dauben' (blue)
Nymphaea 'General Pershing' (pink)
Nymphaea 'Green Smoke' (blue)
Nymphaea 'Hilary' (purple)
Nymphaea 'Jack Wood' (red)
Nymphaea 'Leopardess' (blue)
Nymphaea 'Marion Strawn' (white)
Nymphaea 'Midnight' (purple)
Nymphaea 'Peach Blow' (orangish)
Nymphaea 'Wood's Blue Goddess' (blue)
Nymphaea 'Yellow Dazzler' (yellow)

Night-blooming Tropical Waterlilies
Nymphaea 'Emily Grant Hutchings' (pink)
Nymphaea 'Juno' (white)
Nymphaea 'Missouri' (white)
Nymphaea 'Mrs. George C. Hitchcock' (pink)
Nymphaea 'Sturtevantii' (pink)
Nymphaea 'Wood's White Knight' (white)

Hardy Waterlilies with Changeable Flower Colors
Nymphaea 'Aurora' (yellow to red)
Nymphaea 'Cherokee' (orange to red)
Nymphaea 'Comanche' (yellow to orange)

Nymphaea 'Indiana' (orange to red)
Nymphaea 'JCN Forestier' (yellow-orange to yellow)
Nymphaea 'Paul Hariot' (orange to red)
Nymphaea 'Sioux' (yellow-orange to yellow)

Hardy Waterlilies for Tubs and Containers
Nymphaea 'Chrysantha' (yellow)
Nymphaea 'Helvola' (yellow)
Nymphaea 'Laydekeri Rosea' (pink)

Hardy Waterlilies for Small to Medium Ponds
Nymphaea 'James Brydon' (red)
Nymphaea 'Mary' (pink)
Nymphaea 'Moorei' (yellow)
Nymphaea 'Perry's Baby Red' (red)
Nymphaea 'Walter Pagels' (white)

Hardy Waterlilies for Medium Ponds
Nymphaea 'Anna Epple' (pink)
Nymphaea 'Chubby' (white)
Nymphaea 'Colorado' (orangish)
Nymphaea 'Denver' (yellow)
Nymphaea 'Newton' (red)
Nymphaea 'Pink Sensation' (pink)
Nymphaea 'Pink Sparkle' (pink)
Nymphaea 'Starbright' (white)
Nymphaea 'Venus' (white)
Nymphaea 'Yuh Ling' (pink)

Hardy Waterlilies for Medium to Large Ponds
Nymphaea 'Almost Black' (red)
Nymphaea 'Arc en Ciel' (pink)
Nymphaea 'Atropurpurea' (red)
Nymphaea 'Barbara Dobbins' (orangish)
Nymphaea 'Betsy Sakata' (yellow)
Nymphaea 'Bleeding Heart' (pink)
Nymphaea 'Celebration' (pink)
Nymphaea 'Clyde Ikins' (orangish)
Nymphaea 'Conqueror' (red)
Nymphaea 'Escarboucle' (red)
Nymphaea 'Fabiola' (pink)
Nymphaea 'Florida Sunset' (orangish)

Nymphaea 'Formosa' (pink)
Nymphaea 'Gladstone' (white)
Nymphaea 'Gloire du Temple-sur-Lot' (pink)
Nymphaea 'Gonnère' (white)
Nymphaea 'Hollandia' (pink)
Nymphaea 'Joey Tomocik' (yellow)
Nymphaea 'Laura Strawn' (white)
Nymphaea 'Lily Pons' (pink)
Nymphaea 'Louise Villemarette' (pink)
Nymphaea 'Marliacea Carnea' (pink)
Nymphaea 'Mayla' (pink)
Nymphaea 'Météor' (red)
Nymphaea 'Odorata Gigantea' (white)
Nymphaea 'Peach Glow' (orangish)
Nymphaea 'Peaches and Cream' (orangish)
Nymphaea 'Pink Sunrise' (pink)
Nymphaea 'Queen of Whites' (white)
Nymphaea 'Ray Davies' (pink)
Nymphaea 'Reflected Flame' (orangish)
Nymphaea 'Rose Arey' (pink)
Nymphaea 'Texas Dawn' (yellow)
Nymphaea 'Wow' (pink)
Nymphaea 'Wucai' (red)
Nymphaea 'Ziyu' (red)

Hardy Waterlilies for Large Ponds
Nymphaea 'Attraction' (red)
Nymphaea 'Gold Medal' (yellow)
Nymphaea 'Pöstlingberg' (white)

Marginals for Moist Soil
Bacopa (tropical)
Baldellia ranunculoides f. repens (hardy)
Calla palustris (hardy)
Canna cultivars (tropical)
Cotula coronopifolia (hardy)
Crinum americanum (tropical)
Dichromena (tropical)
Hygrophila corymbosa 'Stricta' (tropical)
Lobelia cardinalis and cultivars (hardy)
Lobelia siphilitica and cultivars (hardy)
Lychnis flos-cuculi (hardy)
Lysimachia nummularia 'Aurea' (hardy)
Mentha aquatica (hardy)
Mimulus guttatus 'Variegatus' (hardy)
Myosotis scorpioides and cultivars (hardy)

Rotala rotundifolia (tropical)
Ruellia brittoniana 'Katie' (tropical)
Wedelia trilobata (tropical)

Marginals for Seasonal Flooding
Alisma plantago-aquatica (hardy)
Apios americana (hardy)
Asclepias (hardy)
Baumea rubiginosa 'Variegata' (hardy)
Caltha palustris (hardy)
Echinodorus cordifolius 'Marble Queen' (hardy)
Epilobium hirsutum (hardy)
Eriophorum vaginatum (hardy)
Hibiscus (hardy)
Hymenocallis liriosome (tropical)
Juncus ensifolius (hardy)
Lilium michiganense (hardy)
Lysichiton americanum (hardy)
Physostegia (hardy)
Ranunculus acris (hardy)
Saururus cernuus (hardy)

Marginals for 2 inches (5 cm) of Water
Carex elata and cultivars (hardy)
Hygrophila difformis (tropical)
Hygrophila difformis 'Variegata' (tropical)
Ludwigia arcuta 'Grandiflora' (hardy)
Ludwigia peploides (tropical)
Lysimachia terrestris (hardy)
Menyanthes trifoliata (hardy)
Oenanthe javanica 'Flamingo' (hardy)

Phyla lanceolata (hardy)
Preslia cervina (hardy)
Ranunculus flammula 'Thor' (hardy)
Sagittaria montevidensis (tropical)
Stachys palustris (hardy)
Veronica (hardy)

Marginals for 6 inches (15 cm) of Water
Acorus calamus 'Variegatus' (hardy)
Colocasia esculenta and cultivars (tropical)
Mimulus alatus (hardy)
Mimulus ringens (hardy)
Orontium aquaticum (hardy)
Sagittaria latifolia and cultivars (hardy)
Saururus chinensis (hardy)
Sium suave (hardy)
Thalia dealbata and cultivars (hardy)

Marginals for 10 inches (25 cm) of Water
Canna 'Erebus' (tropical)
Canna 'Ra' (tropical)
Justicia americana (hardy)
Ludwigia peruviana (tropical)
Pontederia cordata and cultivars (hardy)
Sagittaria lancifolia (tropical)
Thalia geniculata (tropical)

Marginals for 18 inches (45 cm) of Water
Cephalanthus occidentalis (hardy)

HARDY WATERLILIES

All hardy waterlilies (genus *Nymphaea*) are day blooming. Their flowers open in the morning—the precise hour depending upon the climate, season, and cultivar—and then close in mid to late afternoon. Flower colors range from very dark garnet-red to yellow, peach, pink, and clear pristine white. The only colors not found in hardy waterlilies are blues and purples. Roughly a dozen hardy waterlilies have flowers that change color from day to day regardless of the season. This group is called changeable.

Red hardy waterlilies generally bloom earlier and longer than do the other color groups. Those with very deep, dark red petals are especially sensitive to direct sunlight; if they absorb too much of it, their petals overheat and dissolve. Such selections grow best in part shade, with protection from the hot midday sun.

White waterlilies tolerate shade and flower well with less sunlight than the reds, only four or five hours per day. They are usually the first waterlilies to stop flowering in fall as the water starts to cool.

Pink hardy waterlilies usually appear later in the spring than other colors. They generally go dormant about the same time as white waterlilies. Most pink hardy waterlilies have a red or burgundy flush to their leaves, especially in spring, adding to their ornamental value in the water garden. Few pink waterlilies tolerate shade.

Many yellow hardy waterlilies need warmer water than other hardy waterlilies. Yellow hardies also tolerate some shade. Most of them begin to grow in late spring and start flowering in early summer. They continue flowering until fall, often staying open later in the season than the pinks and whites, and almost as late as the red hardies.

Unlike changeable waterlilies, which may have a peach hue for a few hours or a day, truly peach hardy waterlilies retain consistent color throughout the life of each blossom. Some cultivars change color depending on the water temperature of the pond. Peach hardy waterlilies generally start growing in late spring and remain in flower until late fall.

All hardy waterlilies need protection from a freeze. Compared to terrestrial perennials, they are just as easy to grow and need little care or attention. For the effort of an hour or so a week during the summer, waterlily gardeners are rewarded with many weeks of flowers and lush, green growth.

Plant Parts and Habit

Hardy waterlilies grow from underground swollen stems called rhizomes. New leaves and flowers sprout from the tip. Roots, often thick and fleshy, also grow from the rhizome. The larger retractor roots hold the plant in place, and the thinner ones absorb nutrients from the soil and water.

The leaves use long "stems," actually petioles, to reach and float on the water surface. Their uppersides are glossy, green, and leathery, sometimes with brown or dark purple markings. Their undersides are often slightly hairy and may be green, reddish, brown, or even slightly purplish. Roundish and smooth-edged, the leaves are 1–12 inches (2.5–30 cm) wide, depending upon the species or cultivar. All have a single split, called a sinus, which runs from the outer edge to the middle of the leaf, where it joins the petiole. In some selections this cleft is straight and matches exactly, so that it seals precisely. In other cultivars, the cleft is concave, convex, or overlapping. These distinctions aid in the proper identification of the more than 400 cultivars.

The flowers also usually float on the water surface, although some may stand above it.

Opposite: Hardy waterlily *Nymphaea* 'Arc en Ciel' features a beautiful flower and foliage streaked in pink, red, white, and green.

Older cultivars, as well as the species, generally have only a single flower in bloom on any given day. More recent selections may have up to six or seven flowers open at one time. The flowers are generally classified as star-shaped, rounded, peony-shaped, or some variation of these. Petal count may range from 12 to more than 100. The outer sepals are usually green. In succeeding inward rows these change color gradually and transform from green sepals to colored petals.

Landscape Uses

Waterlilies are the color palette of the pond. They grow in the deeper water and in the main body of the pond, but can also be used along the edge of earth-bottom ponds beyond the marginal zone. In this position they can alter the shape of the open water, changing a flat edge into an undulating landscape. Waterlilies are best used in water 3–6 feet (1.8 m) deep in natural ponds and 6–36 inches (15–90 cm) deep in lined ponds.

Optimal Growing Conditions

Sun: Usually six or more hours of direct sunlight each day. Some plants will flower in part shade with between four and six hours of sunlight daily. None grow in dense shade with less than three hours of sunlight every day.

Wind tolerance: Mild. Wind becomes a problem when it causes large ripples on the water.

Water depth: 18–30 inches (45–75 cm) deep for most cultivars, 6 inches (15 cm) deep for miniature and dwarf cultivars, up to 48 inches (120 cm) deep or more for very large cultivars.

Soil and water chemistry: Neutral to slightly alkaline.

Temperature: Warm air and water. Yellow waterlilies need water temperature above 75°F (24°C). Red lilies need cooler water.

Salt tolerance: Very little.

Seasonal Care

Hardy waterlilies rely on the number of hours of sunlight to tell them when they should start growing in the spring or stop growing in the fall.

Spring: Bring submerged plants up to the warmer water at the surface of the pond. Fertilize them when they start to show some floating leaves and the water temperature is above 65°F (18°C).

Summer: Feed plants regularly, generally about once a month. Remove and discard spent flowers and aging leaves.

Fall: Trim old foliage, but do not remove any thin, transparent "indicator leaves" that may develop on some cultivars; these remain underwater at the base of the plant throughout the winter.

Winter: Submerge plants to a depth in the pond where they will not freeze, or remove them from the water garden and keep them cool, dark, and damp. In warmer climates where the water does not freeze, allow plants to go dormant in the pond.

Planting

Hardy waterlilies may be planted dormant when they have little or no leaves or roots, or they may be planted when in active growth with leaves and roots that have already sprouted. To plant a hardy lily, fill the pot about two-thirds full of potting soil. Make a mound in the middle of the pot with a handful of soil. Place the rhizome on the mound in the middle of the pot. Spread out any roots so that they are on top of the soil and out from under the rhizome. Sprinkle soil over the roots and around the rhizome, and then add more soil so that the rhizome is just covered with soil. Try to bury the entire rhizome under just less than 1 inch (2.5 cm) or so of soil, since more soil will make sprouting new leaves more difficult. Water the pot thoroughly, and then add pea gravel around the rhizome, just enough to cover it.

Waterlilies are extremely buoyant when in leaf, but even dormant rhizomes have been known to suddenly pop out of the soil and float on the water surface. If planting the lilies when they are actively growing, try to retain as many roots as possible and anchor them firmly in the soil. Larger lilies may need to be helped for the first week or so, by placing a smooth rock on top of the soil over the rhizome.

Nymphaea 'Almost Black'

Black, cherry-soda red. Peony-shaped blooms of 8–9 inches (20–23 cm). Dark green leaves. Grows to 6–12 feet (1.8–3.6 m) wide in full sun in 6–48 inches (15–120 cm) of water. Good for medium to large ponds. Red color is prone to melt in full sun in summer.

Nymphaea 'Anna Epple'

Baby pink. Cup- or peony-shaped blooms of 4 inches (10 cm). A good bloomer. Green leaves with red tint at edges. Grows to 2–6 feet (60–180 cm) wide in full sun in 6–24 inches (15–60 cm) of water. Good for medium ponds.

Nymphaea 'Arc en Ciel'

White with a hint of pink. Star-shaped blooms of 5–6 inches (13–15 cm). Highly mottled leaves. Grows to 4–5 feet (1.2–1.5 m) wide in full sun to shade in 6–24 inches (15–60 cm) of water. Good for medium or large ponds.

Nymphaea 'Atropurpurea'

Deep red. Bowl-shaped blooms of 7–8 inches (18–20 cm). Purple new leaves that age to green. Grows to more than 4 feet (1.2 m) wide in full sun in 6–36 inches (15–90 cm) of water. Color best in part shade where petals are protected from hot midday sun. Good for medium or large ponds. Earned Royal Horticultural Society Award of Garden Merit in 1906.

Nymphaea 'Almost Black'

Nymphaea 'Anna Epple'

Nymphaea 'Arc en Ciel'

Nymphaea 'Atropurpurea'

Nymphaea 'Attraction'

Nymphaea 'Attraction'

Dark, watermelon red. Goblet-shaped blooms of 10–12 inches (25–30 cm). Green leaves. Grows to 4–5 feet (1.2–1.5 m) wide in full sun in 6–48 inches (15–120 cm) of water. Good for large ponds. Many forms of 'Attraction' are now sold. Some are close to the original description and some are not.

Nymphaea 'Aurora'

Changeable from creamy yellow to orange to dark red. Cup-shaped blooms of 4–4-1/2 inches (10–11 cm). Green leaves blotched purple or maroon. Grows to 3 feet (90 cm) wide in full sun in 6–24 inches (15–60 cm) of water. Good for tub or small ponds.

Nymphaea 'Barbara Dobbins'

Peach to pale yellow with deeper pink blush. Goblet-shaped blooms of 4–8 inches (10–20 cm). Mottled leaves. Grows to 6–8 feet (1.8–2.5 m) wide in full sun in 6–24 inches (15–60 cm) of water. Good for medium or large ponds. Is pink-yellow in spring and fall, but pink in summer.

Nymphaea 'Betsy Sakata'

Soft lemon yellow. Goblet-shaped blooms of 4–6 inches (10–15 cm). Green leaves with small purple flecks. Grows to 3–5 feet (90–150 cm) wide in full sun in 6–36 inches (15–90 cm) of water. Good for medium or large ponds.

Nymphaea 'Barbara Dobbins'

Nymphaea 'Betsy Sakata'

Nymphaea 'Aurora'

Nymphaea 'Black Opal'

Deep red. Goblet-shaped blooms of 3–5 inches (7.5–13 cm). Burgundy foliage fades to a deep maroon-green. Grows to 3–5 feet (90–150 cm) wide in full sun to part shade in 6–30 inches (15–75 cm) of water. Good for small to medium ponds.

Nymphaea 'Bleeding Heart'

Very, very pink that is almost red. Goblet- or peony-shaped blooms of 4–6 inches (10–15 cm). Bright green leaves. Grows 3–5 feet (90–150 cm) wide in full sun in 6–36 inches (15–90 cm) of water. Good for medium to large ponds.

Nymphaea 'Celebration'

Very intense rose pink. Peony-shaped blooms of 5–6 inches (13–15 cm). Deep green leaves. Grows to 6–12 feet (1.8–3.6 m) wide in full sun in 6–24 inches (15–60 cm) of water. Good for medium or large ponds.

Nymphaea 'Cherokee'

Changeable, opening orange, turning redder each day until it becomes a glassy, candy-apple red. Blooms of 3–5 inches (7.5–13 cm). Green leaves brushed in purple. Grows 3–4 feet (90–120 cm) wide in 6–30 inches (15–75 cm) of water. Good for containers and small to medium ponds.

Nymphaea 'Black Opal'

Nymphaea 'Bleeding Heart'

Nymphaea 'Chromatella'

Nymphaea 'Chromatella'

Canary yellow. Goblet-shaped blooms of 4–6 inches (10–15 cm). Olive-green leaves with bronze markings. Grows to 6–12 feet (1.8–3.6 m) wide in full sun to part shade in 6–48 inches (15–120 cm) of water. Good for any size pond, from small to earth bottom. Earned Royal Horticultural Society Award of Garden Merit in 1895. Flowers reliably in cool weather.

Nymphaea 'Celebration'

Nymphaea 'Cherokee'

Nymphaea 'Chrysantha'

Chrome-yellow. Star-shaped blooms of 5–6 inches (13–15 cm). Green leaves with purple flecks. Grows to 6–24 inches (15–60 cm) wide in full sun in 6–24 inches (15–60 cm) of water. Good for small or medium ponds and containers.

Nymphaea 'Chubby'

Creamy white. Peony-shaped blooms of 4 inches (10 cm). Green leaves with red tint at edges. Grows to 2–6 feet (60–180 cm) wide in full sun in 6–24 inches (15–60 cm) of water. Good for medium ponds.

Nymphaea 'Clyde Ikins'

Peach, even on the golden side of cantaloupe. Ball- or goblet-shaped blooms of 8–9 inches (20– 23 cm). Green, flecked leaves. Grows to 6–12 feet (1.8–3.6 m) wide in full sun in 6–24 inches (15–60 cm) or more of water. Slow to spread or increase. Good for medium or large ponds. Stays peach from spring through fall.

Nymphaea 'Colorado'

Peach, starting yellow with pink in spring, turning smoked salmon in summer. Star-shaped blooms of 4–6 inches (10–15 cm). New leaves are mottled in burgundy, maturing to green. Grows to 4–6 feet (1.2–1.8 m) wide in full sun to part shade in 6–36 inches (15–90 cm) of water. Good for medium ponds. Longer flowering than most waterlilies, continuing to flower even after all its foliage has died back for winter.

Nymphaea 'Chrysantha'

Nymphaea 'Chubby'

Nymphaea 'Clyde Ikins'

Nymphaea 'Colorado'

Nymphaea 'Comanche'

Changeable, from pale yellow to pale orange. Peony-shaped blooms of 3–5 inches (7.5–13 cm). Freckled leaves. Grows to 3–5 feet (90–150 cm) wide in full sun in 6–20 inches (15–50 cm) of water. Good for small or medium ponds.

Nymphaea 'Conqueror'

Watermelon red on white. Goblet-shaped blooms of 6–8 inches (15–20 cm). Grows to 6–8 feet (1.8–2.5 m) wide in full sun in 6–48 inches (15–120 cm) of water. Good for medium or large ponds.

Nymphaea 'Comanche'

Nymphaea 'Denver'

White-yellow. Peony-shaped blooms of 4 inches (10 cm). Green leaves with red tint at edges. Grows to 2–6 feet (60–180 cm) wide in full sun in 6–24 inches (15–60 cm) of water. Good for medium ponds.

Nymphaea 'Escarboucle'

Deep cherry red. Cup-shaped blooms of 6–7 inches (15–18 cm). Green leaves. Grows to 4–5 feet (1.2–1.5 m) wide in full sun in 6–48 inches (15–120 cm) of water. Good for medium or large ponds. Earned Royal Horticultural Society Award of Garden Merit in 1993.

Nymphaea 'Fabiola'

Bubblegum pink. Star-shaped blooms of 4 inches (10 cm). Green leaves with red undersides. Grows to 6–12 feet (1.8–3.6 m) wide in full sun in 6–24 inches (15–60 cm) of water. Good for medium or large ponds.

Nymphaea 'Florida Sunset'

Peach or yellow with pink and orange. Ball- or goblet-shaped blooms of 8–9 inches (20–23 cm). Green leaves flecked with brown. Grows to 6–12 feet (1.8–3.6 m) wide in full sun in 6–48 inches (15–120 cm) of water. Good for medium or large ponds.

Nymphaea 'Conqueror'

Nymphaea 'Denver'

Nymphaea 'Escarboucle'

Nymphaea 'Florida Sunset'

Nymphaea 'Fabiola'

Nymphaea 'Formosa'

Pale, chiffon pink. Open, cup-shaped blooms of 3–5 inches (7.5–13 cm). Green leaves. Grows to 3–5 feet (90–150 cm) wide in full sun in 6–36 inches (15–90 cm) of water. Good for medium or large ponds.

Nymphaea 'Gladstone'

Snow white. Goblet- or cup-shaped blooms of 4–6 inches (10–15 cm). Dark green leaves. Grows to 6–12 feet (1.8–3.6 m) or more wide in full sun in 6–48 inches (15–120 cm) or more of water. Good for medium or large ponds.

Nymphaea 'Gloire du Temple-sur-Lot'

Pale but very pink. Ball- or peony-shaped blooms of 6 inches (15 cm). Green leaves. Grows to 6–12 feet (1.8–3.6 m) wide in full sun in 6–24 inches (15–60 cm) of water. Good for medium or large ponds.

Nymphaea 'Gold Medal'

Strong golden yellow. Goblet-shaped blooms of 6–8 inches (15–20 cm). Green leaves. Grows to 4–6 feet (1.2–1.8 m) wide in full sun in 6–48 inches (15–120 cm) or more of water. Good for large ponds.

Nymphaea 'Formosa'

Nymphaea 'Gloire du Temple-sur-Lot'

Nymphaea 'Gladstone'

Nymphaea 'Gold Medal'

Nymphaea 'Gonnère'

Snow white. Ball- or peony-shaped blooms of 4–6 inches (10–15 cm). Pea-green leaves. Grows to 4–6 feet (1.2–1.8 m) wide in full sun in 6–30 inches (15–75 cm) of water. Good for medium or large ponds. Synonyms *Nymphaea* 'Crystal White', *N.* 'Snowball'. Earned Royal Horticultural Society Award of Garden Merit in 1993.

Nymphaea 'Helvola'

Light lemon yellow. Small, star-shaped bloom of 1–2 inches (2.5–5 cm). Green leaves freckled with burgundy. Grows to 1–3 feet (30–90 cm) wide in full sun in 1–12 inches (2.5–30 cm) of water. Good for containers or small ponds.

Nymphaea 'Hollandia'

White with red dots for a pink look. Peony-shaped blooms of 5–6 inches (13–15 cm). Grows to 6–12 feet (1.8–3.6 m) wide in full sun in 6–24 inches (15–60 cm) of water. Good for medium or large ponds. Synonym *Nymphaea* 'Darwin'.

Nymphaea 'Indiana'

Changeable red, yellow, and orange. Cup-shaped blooms of 2–3 inches (5–7.5 cm). Green leaves with red spots. Grows to 1–3 feet (30–90 cm) wide in full sun in 6–24 inches (15–60 cm) of water. Good for small ponds or containers.

Nymphaea 'Helvola'

Nymphaea 'Gonnère'

Nymphaea 'Indiana'

Nymphaea 'Hollandia'

Nymphaea 'James Brydon'

Unique red to rose pink. Ball- or peony-shaped blooms of 4–6 inches (10–15 cm). Green leaves. Grows to 4–12 feet (1.2–3.6 m) wide in full sun to part shade in 6–48 inches (15–120 cm) of water. Tolerates more shade than most. Good for small to large ponds. Earned Royal Horticultural Society Award of Garden Merit in 1993.

Nymphaea 'JCN Forestier'

Creamy yellow with red and orange highlights. Cup-shaped blooms of 4–8 inches (10–20 cm). Peppered leaves. Grows to 6–12 feet (1.8–3.6 m) wide in full sun in 6–48 inches (15–120 cm) of water. Good for medium or large ponds.

Nymphaea 'Joey Tomocik'

Canary yellow. Loose, star-shaped blooms of 4–6 inches (10–15 cm). Speckled leaves. Grows 6–10 feet (1.8–3 m) in full sun to part shade in 6–40 inches (15–100 cm) of water. Good for medium or large ponds. One of the earliest yellow waterlilies to bloom.

Nymphaea 'James Brydon'

Nymphaea 'JCN Forestier'

Nymphaea 'Laura Strawn'

Nymphaea 'Laura Strawn'

Creamy off-white. Very cup- and almost mug-shaped blooms of 6–8 inches (15–20 cm). Grows to 6–12 feet (1.8–3.6 m) wide in full sun in 6–48 inches (15–120 cm) of water. Good for medium or large ponds.

Nymphaea 'Laydekeri Rosea'

Washed-out red. Open, cup-shaped blooms of 2–4 inches (5–10 cm). Green leaves with red edges. Grows to 1–3 feet (30–90 cm) wide in full sun in 6–24 inches (15–60 cm) of water. Good for small ponds or containers.

Nymphaea 'Joey Tomocik'

Nymphaea 'Laydekeri Rosea'

Nymphaea 'Lily Pons'

Nymphaea 'Louise Villemarette'

Nymphaea 'Lily Pons'

Bubblegum pink. Ball- or peony-shaped blooms of 6–8 inches (15–20 cm). Green leaves. Grows to 4–6 feet (1.2–1.8 m) wide in full sun in 6–48 inches (15–120 cm) of water. Good for medium or large ponds.

Nymphaea 'Louise Villemarette'

Soft pink. Cup-shaped blooms of 3–5 inches (7.5–13 cm). Green leaves. Grows to 4–6 feet (1.2–1.8 m) wide in full sun in 6–48 inches (15–120 cm) of water. Good for medium or large ponds.

Nymphaea 'Marliacea Carnea'

White with red flares. Cup-shaped blooms of 4–6 inches (10–15 cm). Green leaves. Grows to 6–8 feet (1.8–2.5 m) wide in full sun to part shade in 6–48 inches (15–120 cm) of water. Good for medium or large ponds.

Nymphaea 'Mary'

Very rosy, almost red. Peony- or cup-shaped blooms of 4–6 inches (10–15 cm). Green leaves. Grows to 3–6 feet (90–180 cm) wide in full sun in 6–36 inches (15–90 cm) of water. Good for small or medium ponds. Flowers reliably in Zone 8 and southward.

Nymphaea 'Mary'

Nymphaea 'Marliacea Carnea'

Nymphaea 'Mayla'

Nymphaea 'Moorei'

Nymphaea 'Newton'

Nymphaea 'Météor'

Nymphaea 'Mayla'

Deep rose pink. Peony-shaped blooms of 5–6 inches (13–15 cm). Deep green leaves. Grows to 6–12 feet (1.8–3.6 m) wide in full sun in 6–24 inches (15–60 cm) of water. Good for medium or large ponds.

Nymphaea 'Météor'

Red. Flat, peony-shaped blooms of 5–6 inches (13–15 cm). Green leaves flecked and shaded with red and with red undersides. Grows to 4–6 feet (1.2–1.8 m) wide in full sun in 6–36 inches (15–90 cm) of water. Good for medium or large ponds.

Nymphaea 'Moorei'

Yellow. Goblet-shaped blooms of 3–5 inches (7.5–13 cm). Green leaves. Grows to 3–5 feet (90–150 cm) in full sun in 6–24 inches (15–60 cm) of water. Good for small or medium ponds. Synonym *Nymphaea* 'Mooreana'.

Nymphaea 'Newton'

Red with a hint of orange. Star- or cup-shaped blooms of 4–6 inches (10–15 cm). Green leaves with purple mottling. Grows to 3–5 feet (90–150 cm) wide in full sun in 6–36 inches (15–90 cm) of water. Good for medium ponds.

Nymphaea 'Odorata Gigantea'

Snow white to creamy. Cup- or goblet-shaped blooms of 4–8 inches (10–20 cm). Green leaves. Grows to 4–6 feet (1.2–1.8 m) in full sun to part shade in 6–72 inches (15–180 cm) of water. Good for medium or large ponds. Synonym *Nymphaea odorata* 'Aiton'.

Nymphaea 'Paul Hariot'

Changeable orange and red. Cup-shaped blooms of 2–3 inches (5–7.5 cm). Green leaves. Grows to 1–3 feet (30–90 cm) wide in full sun in 6–24 inches (15–60 cm) of water. Good for small ponds and containers.

Nymphaea 'Paul Hariot'

Nymphaea 'Odorata Gigantea'

Nymphaea 'Peach Glow'

Nymphaea 'Peaches and Cream'

Nymphaea 'Perry's Baby Red'

Nymphaea 'Pink Sensation'

Nymphaea 'Peach Glow'

Peach or orange-pink. Goblet-shaped blooms of 6 inches (12 mm) or more. Green leaves with faint mottling. Grows to 3–5 feet (90–150 cm) wide in full sun in 6–36 inches (15–90 cm) of water. Good for medium or large ponds.

Nymphaea 'Peaches and Cream'

Peach. Peony-shaped blooms of 6–8 inches (15–20 cm). Green leaves, purple-speckled when young. Grows to 4–6 feet (1.2–1.8 m) wide in full sun in 6–48 inches (15–120 cm) of water. Good for medium or large ponds. Flower color turns to yellow and deep pink in summer when the water temperature rises above 70–75°F (21–24°C).

Nymphaea 'Perry's Baby Red'

Deep red. Cup- or ball-shaped blooms of 2–4 inches (5–10 cm). Medium to dark green leaves. Grows to 2–4 feet (60–120 cm) wide in full sun to part shade in 4–12 inches (10–30 cm) of water. Good for small ponds. Cold hardy to Zone 4 but flowers reliably in Zone 8 and southward.

Nymphaea 'Pink Sensation'

Rosy pink. Star- or cup-shaped blooms of 4–6 inches (10–15 cm). Green leaves. Grows to 3–5

Nymphaea 'Pink Sparkle'

Nymphaea 'Pink Sunrise'

feet (90–150 cm) wide in full sun in 6–24 inches (15–60 cm) of water. Good for medium ponds.

Nymphaea 'Pink Sparkle'
Silvery pink. Cup-shaped blooms of 4–6 inches (10–15 cm). Green leaves 10–12 inches (25–30 cm) across. Grows to 3–5 feet (90–150 cm) wide in full sun in 6–24 inches (15–60 cm) of water. Good for medium ponds.

Nymphaea 'Pink Sunrise'
Grapefruit pink. Peony-shaped blooms of 5–8 inches (13–20 cm). Flecked, green leaves. Grows to 6–12 feet (1.8–3.6 m) wide in full sun in 6–24 inches (15–60 cm) or more of water. Good for medium or large ponds.

Nymphaea 'Pöstlingberg'

Nymphaea 'Pöstlingberg'
Off-white. Cup-shaped blooms of 6–7 inches (15–18 cm). Green leaves. Grows to 6 feet (1.8 m) wide in full sun in 6–48 inches (15–120 cm) of water. Good for large ponds.

Nymphaea 'Queen of Whites'
Clean, crisp white. Goblet-shaped blooms of 4–6 inches (10–15 cm). Green leaves. Grows to 4–8 feet (1.2–2.5 m) wide in full sun to part shade in 6–48 inches (15–120 cm) or more of water. Good for medium or large ponds.

Nymphaea 'Queen of Whites'

Nymphaea 'Reflected Flame'

Nymphaea 'Ray Davies'

Nymphaea 'Rose Arey'

Nymphaea 'Ray Davies'

Rose pink. Goblet-shaped blooms of 4–6 inches (10–15 cm). Green leaves. Grows to 4–8 feet (1.2–2.5 m) wide in full sun in 6–36 inches (15–90 cm) of water. Good for medium or large ponds.

Nymphaea 'Reflected Flame'

Cream with a pinky peach blush. Star-shaped blooms of 4–6 inches (10–15 cm). Green leaves with faint mottling. Grows to 4–6 feet (1.2–1.8 m) wide in full sun in 6–48 inches (15–120 cm) of water. Good for medium or large ponds.

Nymphaea 'Rose Arey'

Soft, baby pink. Star- or cup-shaped blooms of 4–6 inches (10–15 cm). Green leaves with a purple cast. Grows to 4–5 feet (1.2–1.5 m) wide in full sun in 6–36 inches (15–90 cm) of water. Good for medium or large ponds.

Nymphaea 'Sioux'

Changeable creamy yellow with red and orange blushing. Cup-shaped blooms of 3–4 inches (7.5–10 cm). Mottled leaves. Grows to 3–5 feet (90–150 cm) wide in full sun in 6–20 inches (15–50 cm) of water. Good for medium or large pond.

Nymphaea 'Sioux'

Nymphaea 'Wucai'

Nymphaea 'Yuh Ling'

Nymphaea 'Wucai'

Watermelon red that is more red in summer than spring. Cup-shaped blooms of 4–6 inches (10–15 cm). Green leaves with a red flush. Grows to 6–8 feet (1.8–2.5 m) wide in full sun in 6–24 inches (15–60 cm) of water. Good for medium or large ponds. Because the red flower has some white in its pigment, it is not likely to melt in full sun.

Nymphaea 'Yuh Ling'

Pale pink. Star- or cup-shaped blooms of 4–6 inches (10–15 cm). Dark green leaves. Grows to 2–6 feet (60–180 cm) wide in full sun in 6–24 inches (15–60 cm) of water. Good for medium ponds.

Nymphaea 'Ziyu'

Watermelon red. Cup-shaped blooms of 4–6 inches (10–15 cm). Green leaves. Grows to 6–8 feet (1.8–2.5 m) wide in full sun in 6–24 inches (15–60 cm) of water. Good for medium or large ponds.

Nymphaea 'Ziyu' backed by *Orontium aquaticum*

TROPICAL WATERLILIES

Tropical waterlilies (genus *Nymphaea*) captivate the hearts of gardeners of all ages and experience. Pond keepers in warmer climates make their first water features big enough to hold at least one of these hot-blooded beauties. Gardeners in colder climates may at first hesitate to grow tropical waterlilies, since they cannot overwinter in the outdoor pond. Once these gardeners see a tropical lily's enchanting color and get a whiff of its heady fragrance, they are quick to change their minds.

Plant Parts and Habit

Unlike many hardy waterlilies, which grow from creeping rhizomes, tropicals grow upright from a central crown, looking much like a pineapple. Their leaves are like those of hardy lilies except for the edge, which in tropical lilies is jagged. Their flowers are magnificent and huge, reaching more than 12 inches (30 cm) in diameter. The plants often have seven or more blooms open at a time. Like hardy waterlilies, tropical waterlilies come in a range of flower colors, from white to red, yellow, blue, lavender, and even purple. Their fragrance can be anything from soft vanilla to spicy ginger or fruity citrus. Even their foliage adds color and sparkle to the pond. Leaves are often speckled or streaked in brown, maroon, or purple. Most cultivars now sold bloom during daylight hours, but some only bloom at night. New spotted flower forms are becoming available, as are new multi- or double-flowered forms.

Landscape Uses

Tropical waterlilies often have a wide leaf spread, making them suitable for ponds that are 8 feet (2.5 m) or more in diameter and at least 6 inches (15 cm) deep. Because they will not overwinter in colder climates, they can be grown in shallower water that tends to heat up sooner. One or two in a wide, open pond makes a truly stunning display for weeks on end. Few if any additional water plants are needed to complete the scene.

Fortunately, some cultivars are suitable for smaller water gardens, and a few will even grow well in a container pond that is only a few feet wide. Placed near a doorway or the outside patio table, their sweet fragrance is carried along on the slightest breeze. Smaller cultivars grow well in small to medium ponds with a capacity to 4000 gallons (15,000 liters) of water. Larger cultivars can be used as annuals in lakes and very large lined ponds.

Optimal Growing Conditions

Sun: Eight or more hours of direct sunlight each day. In warmer climates, where daytime temperatures reach or exceed 100°F (35°C) for 10 days or more, most tropical waterlilies appreciate a few hours of morning shade.

Wind tolerance: None. Wind that causes continuous wave action is detrimental, as is water splashing on the leaves from waterfalls, fountains, and the like.

Water depth: Usually 12–24 inches (30–60 cm) deep, as little as 6 inches (15 cm) for small plants, up to as much as 48 inches (120 cm) for larger plants. Not suitable for ponds with substantial changes in water depth, such as irrigation ponds.

Soil and water chemistry: Neutral to slightly acidic.

Temperature: Hot air; hot water from 70°F (21°C) to above 80°F (27°C).

Salt tolerance: None.

Seasonal Care

Spring: Place plants in the outdoor pond when the water reaches a consistent temperature of about 70°F (21°C). Begin to fertilize them every two or three weeks.

Opposite: A pink-flowered tropical waterlily blooms in the center of a fish-stocked pond.

Summer: Remove old flowers and yellow or faded leaves. In very warm weather, fertilize heavily blooming plants more often.

Winter: Leave plants outdoors in ponds where the water temperature does not fall below 60°F (16°C). In colder areas where frost is an issue, bring plants indoors. Cultivars that do not form dormant tubers must be overwintered in water; other selections may be dried down and stored as dormant tubers.

Planting

A dormant tuber can be simply planted in the middle of a pot filled about two-thirds full with cat litter or heavy clay soil—nothing with added organic matter—that has been mixed with a granular fertilizer. Plant the tuber about 1–3 inches (2.5–7.5 cm) below the soil surface. The tuber sends sprouts up to the surface, as many as 18 in some tubers, resulting in 18 plants.

Start small waterlilies in quart (liter) or 4-inch (10-cm) pots. When they have filled that out, or if they have larger crowns, use a 7-gallon (26-liter) pot. Tropical waterlilies are heavy feeders and those for larger ponds appreciate a pot with a lot of room.

When in active growth, tropical waterlilies do not have a well-defined tuber. Instead, their roots and crown look more like a bare-root impatiens plant. To plant the lily, fill the pot about two-thirds full of soil, making a slight mound in the middle. Place the lily on top of the mound, spreading out its roots across the soil. The stems of the lily leaves will generally be light colored where they emerge from the base of the plant and darker colored a few inches away from the base. The point at which light changes to dark shows the soil line where the leaves of the lily were planted below the soil surface. Try to match that depth, or plant them at a more shallow depth.

Tropical waterlilies float very easily when they have started to sprout roots and leaves. To keep them in their pots, leave some roots so they can help anchor the plant in the soil. Place a smooth rock on top of the soil over the roots for the first

Nymphaea 'Blue Beauty'

week or so to keep larger lilies in place. Or, use string to crisscross the crown and foliage to anchor the plant in the pot. New roots grow quickly once the lily is in warm water, often rooting into the pot in about a week.

Nymphaea 'Albert Greenburg'

Day-blooming in a mix of pink, yellow, and orange. Cup-shaped blooms of 8 inches (20 cm). Mottled green leaves. Spread of 6-1/2 feet (2 m). Good for medium to large ponds. Will bloom with as little as four hours of sun.

Nymphaea 'Blue Beauty'

Day-blooming in lilac-blue. Cup-shaped blooms of 8–10 inches (20–25 cm) with a spicy perfume. Dark green leaves speckled with brown. Spread of 6-1/2 feet (2 m). Good for large ponds or containers.

Nymphaea colorata

Day-blooming in purple-blue-violet. Pinwheel-shaped blooms of 3–4 inches (7.5–10 cm). Green leaves. Spread of 2–3 feet (60–90 cm). Good for small to medium ponds and containers.

Nymphaea 'Dauben'

Day-blooming in creamy white with lavender tips. Star-shaped, fragrant blooms of 2–4 inches (5–10 cm). Green leaves. Spread of 1–8 feet (30–250 cm). Good for small to medium ponds and containers. Highly viviparous. Synonym *Nymphaea* 'Daubeniana'.

Nymphaea 'Emily Grant Hutchings'

Night-blooming in rose pink. Cup-shaped blooms of 10 inches (25 cm). Bronze leaves. Spread of 6-1/2 feet (2 m). Good for medium to large ponds.

Nymphaea 'Albert Greenburg'

Nymphaea colorata

Nymphaea 'Dauben'

Nymphaea 'Emily Grant Hutchings'

Nymphaea 'General Pershing'

Day-blooming in orchid pink, opening early and closing late. Platter-shaped, deeply fragrant, double blooms of 8–10 inches (20–25 cm). Dark green leaves mottled with purple. Spread of 6-1/2 feet (2 m). Good for medium to large ponds.

Nymphaea 'Green Smoke'

Day-blooming in chartreuse with smoky blue tips. Platter-shaped blooms of 6–8 inches (15–20 cm). Lightly speckled, bronze-green leaves. Spread of 5–6 feet (1.5–1.8 m). Good for small to medium ponds.

Nymphaea 'General Pershing'

Nymphaea 'Jack Wood'

Nymphaea 'Green Smoke'

Nymphaea 'Hilary'

Day-blooming in pale lavender. Cup- or star-shaped blooms of 4–6 inches (10–15 cm). Green leaves. Medium spread. Good for medium ponds. Viviparous.

Nymphaea 'Jack Wood'

Day-blooming in raspberry red. Platter-shaped, abundant blooms of 6–8 inches (15–20 cm). Purple-mottled leaves. Spread of 5–6 feet (1.5–1.8 m). Good for small to medium ponds.

Nymphaea 'Hilary'

Nymphaea 'Juno'

Nymphaea 'Leopardess'

Nymphaea 'Lindsey Woods'

Nymphaea 'Marion Strawn'

Nymphaea 'Midnight'

Nymphaea 'Juno'

Night-blooming in creamy white. Star-shaped blooms of 4–6 inches (10–15 cm). Green leaves. Medium to large spread. Good for large ponds.

Nymphaea 'Leopardess'

Day-blooming in cobalt blue. Platter-shaped, highly fragrant blooms of 6–8 inches (15-20 cm). Green leaves heavily mottled with maroon. Spread of 5-1/2 feet (1.6 m). Good for small, medium, or large ponds.

Nymphaea 'Lindsey Woods'

Day-blooming in deep purple. Platter-shaped blooms of 4–6 inches (10–15 cm). Green leaves with purple spots. Medium to large spread. Good for medium to large ponds.

Nymphaea 'Marion Strawn'

Day-blooming in snow white that is slightly gray. Star-shaped blooms of 6 inches (15 cm). Slightly mottled leaves. Spread of 6 feet (1.8 m). Good for medium to large ponds.

Nymphaea 'Midnight'

Day-blooming in purple with gold centers. Star-shaped, double, fragrant blooms of 6 inches (15 cm). Dark green, red-flecked leaves. Spread of 4–5 feet (1.2–1.5 m). Good for small, medium, or large ponds. Free-flowering.

Nymphaea 'Missouri'

Nymphaea 'Missouri'

Night-blooming in creamy white. Star-shaped blooms of 12 inches (30 cm) with broad petals. Green leaves with copper-brown new growth. Spread of 6–7 feet (1.8–2.1 m). Good for large ponds—it gets huge.

Nymphaea 'Mrs. George C. Hitchcock'

Night-blooming in orchid pink, continuing into the fall. Star-shaped blooms of 12 inches (30 cm). Bronze leaves. Spread of 6–7 feet (1.8–2.1 m). Good for medium to large ponds.

Nymphaea 'Peach Blow'

Day-blooming in pink with peach centers. Platter-shaped blooms of 6–10 inches (15–25 cm). Light green leaves with many tiny red flecks. Spread of 6-1/2 feet (2 m). Good for medium to large ponds. Highly viviparous.

Nymphaea 'Pink Perfection'

Day-blooming in bubblegum pink. Platter-shaped, very fragrant blooms of 6 inches (15 cm). Heavily variegated leaves. Large spread. Good for medium to large ponds.

Nymphaea 'Sturtevantii'

Night-blooming in strong pink-edged blooms with pale centers. Star-shaped, heavily scented blooms of 6–10 inches (15–25 cm). Bronze leaves. Medium to large spread. Good for medium ponds.

Nymphaea 'Wood's Blue Goddess'

Day-blooming in powder blue edged in purple. Star-shaped blooms of 6–8 inches (15–20 cm). Green leaves. Medium to large spread. Good for medium to large ponds. Foliage and flowers are odd, similar to those of night bloomers.

Nymphaea 'Mrs. George C. Hitchcock'

Nymphaea 'Peach Blow'

Nymphaea 'Wood's Blue Goddess'

Nymphaea 'Sturtevantii'

Nymphaea 'Pink Perfection'

Nymphaea 'Wood's White Knight'

Nymphaea 'Yellow Dazzler'

Nymphaea 'Wood's White Knight'
Night-blooming in white with yellow stamens. Star-shaped, fragrant blooms of 6–8 inches (15–20 cm). Green leaves. Spread of 6-1/2 feet (2 m). Good for medium to large ponds. Flowers reliably and abundantly.

Nymphaea 'Yellow Dazzler'
Day-blooming in bright yellow. Star-shaped, fragrant blooms of 6 inches (15 cm). Deeply speckled green leaves. Spread of 6-1/2–10 feet (2–3 m). Good for small to medium ponds. Abundant flowers.

LOTUS

Lotus (genus *Nelumbo*) are exotic beauties that grace many public and private water gardens. More than 600 selections and hybrids of *N. nucifera*, the Asian lotus, have been developed, while *N. lutea*, the American lotus, has led to only a few new plants. American hybridizer Perry Slocum has crossed the two species to make free-flowering selections in rich colors not previously known. He has also introduced lotus with blossoms that consistently rise above the foliage—an important trait, since the flowers of many forms of lotus appear among or remain completely hidden underneath the large leaves.

Lotus are available in a wide range of sizes and colors. Some selections grow no more than a foot (30 cm) tall and have flowers no larger than a tennis ball. Others are huge, stately plants, reaching over 6 feet (1.8 m) tall, with leaves more than 2 feet (60 cm) in diameter and flowers as large as a basketball. Fragrance varies from heady and fruity to mild. Colors range from the deepest rosy pink—none are truly red—to the cleanest white, and include some bicolors, changeables, or tones that blush or fade.

Plant Parts and Habit

The center, or heart, of the lotus flower is a disk-shaped cone that holds the seed and pistils. This heart is usually yellow, occasionally green in some selections. Once the flower is spent, the cone gradually changes color, turning a light, tawny brown. Fertile seed becomes enlarged and black, while nonfertilized seed shrivels into the seed head.

Lotus begin to flower several weeks later than waterlilies, often not until mid or late summer, and continue until frost. The flowers open at different times, depending upon their age. First-day blooms usually open around 4 or 5 a.m., staying open for just three or four hours, and then closing around 8 a.m. On the second day, the flower begins to open just after midnight, at about 1 a.m., and by 7 or 8 a.m. will be fully open. Again

it stays open for only a short time, closing around noon that same day. On the third day, the flower again opens in the dark, around 1 a.m., and is fully open by 9 a.m. By noon, it will close, but may not close fully or completely. On the fourth and final day, the flower opens during the morning or afternoon. It will be faded and tattered and will begin to shed its petals.

Lotus foliage is a spectacular sight, especially in the larger selections. Each leaf is round and wavy, with the stem attaching to the leaf's center so that it resembles an inverted parasol. The texture is fine and slightly waxy. The color is usually bright green or slightly bluish green, highlighting the often-lavender undertones of white or pink blossoms. Leaf and flower stems are hairy, almost prickly, and hollow. They exude a white, milky, gooey substance when bent or broken.

Landscape Uses

Lotus are best grown in pots, so their tubers do not overtake the entire water feature. Smaller tub gardens filled with lotus are a perfect accent to an entryway and quickly liven up a drab corner of a backyard patio. Containerized lotus look tropical despite their winter hardiness. Taking the container to its smallest extreme are bowl lotus, sometimes called teacup lotus. These diminutive plants grow to no more than 2 feet (60 cm) tall. Some, in fact, only grow 4 inches (10 cm) tall. They are perfectly happy in a 6-inch (15-cm) pot and need only a few inches of water over their crown. Often they are grown in rice bowls in China. Such miniature lotus gardens need little more than full sunlight and constant moisture. Bowl lotus are lotus in all respects, taking virtually as many forms as full-sized lotus do. They begin to bloom about a month earlier than full-sized lotus, starting their show in early summer. Foliage is a characteristic gray-green, held in velvety circles above the water surface. Tubers are slender and grow a few inches below the soil.

The spectacular leaves, cheerful flowers, and unusual seed heads of lotus add interest to a pond at the Chicago Botanic Garden.

Optimal Growing Conditions

Sun: Usually full sun. A few cultivars will grow and flower in part shade with between five and six hours of sunlight daily.

Wind tolerance: None. Lotus generally can tolerate wave action, such as that from a fountain, as long as the leaves are not constantly being wetted once they no longer lay on the surface of the water.

Water depth: 6–8 inches (15–20 cm) deep above the crown, with large selections tolerating very deep water more than 12 inches (30 cm), or even up to 6 feet (1.8 m), above the crown.

Soil and water chemistry: Organic, rich, clay-like soil from acidic to neutral.

Temperature: Warm, humid summers where the water and soil are between 70°F (21°C) and 86°F (30°C). Even temperatures are best.

Salt tolerance: None.

Seasonal Care

Spring: If plants were overwintered at the bottom on the pond, bring them up to a few inches below the water surface, where they can be warmed by sunlight. If plants were overwintered as dormant bare-root tubers, pot them and place them in the pond when the water temperature is about 65°F (18°C). If tubers were overwintered in a pot in a cooler, return them to the pond as soon as the risk of freezing is past.

Summer: Fertilize blooming plants at least once a month. Keep the pot in full sun for best growth and most blooms. Remove spent leaves and flowers by cutting the stem just above the water surface.

Winter: Protect plants and/or tubers from freezing. In warmer climates, allow plants to slow in growth as day length wanes; they do not need to go dormant.

Planting

Lotus grow best in rounded pots because their tubers, which grow end to end, can become stunted once they encounter a corner in a square or rectangular pot, or may crawl up and out of the pot. Smaller bowl lotus grow well in pots that are only 8–10 inches (20–25 cm) in diameter, though slightly larger, 10–14 inches (25–35 cm) across, is better. Larger cultivars should be potted in containers that are 24 inches (60 cm) wide or more.

The best time of year to pot up lotus is in early spring, when the tubers are dormant or have barely sprouted new growth. Most sources recommend planting bare-root lotus tubers in soil, with the growing tip exposed above the soil surface. We have found this method to be only moderately successful. The Chinese float bare-root lotus tubers in planting pots, allowing plants to sprout and grow before they are put into the soil. This method yields much better success. Fill each pot roughly half full with soil, and then add a few inches of water to the pot. Float a single tuber in the water and keep it warm, between 75°F (24°C) and 86°F (30°C). Place the pot in a sunny location. Change the water every few days to prevent it from fouling and infecting the lotus tuber. Once the plant has sprouted three or four leaves, gently place the tuber on the soil, holding it in place with a flat, smooth rock. As the tuber grows, it develops retractor roots that pull the tuber down into the soil. After the first few floating "coin leaves" are produced, the plant develops aerial leaves on its own (no extra support or decrease in water level is needed). Add more water to the pot as the plant matures. After it has grown six or seven aerial leaves, place the plant in the pond, increasing water depth only gradually.

Lotus leaves are not able to stretch to reach above the water surface. If a tuber has already sprouted a few leaves, do not submerge them in the water. Simply add as much water as will permit the leaves to float on the surface. The plant will sprout more leaves that will be able to stand above the water. The amount of water in the pot may then be increased accordingly. We have found that bowl lotus grow well with just 3–4 inches (10 cm) of soil in the pot and 2–3 inches (5–7.5 cm) of water.

In the descriptions that follow, the spread stated for each plant is based on its performance in a 7-gallon (25-liter) pot. Lotus will spread indefinitely if allowed.

Nelumbo 'Alba Plena'

Nelumbo 'Baiyun Wanlian'

Nelumbo 'Charles Thomas'

Nelumbo 'Carolina Queen'

Nelumbo 'Chawan Basu'

Nelumbo 'Alba Plena'

Snow white. Double blooms of 8–10 inches (20–25 cm). Height 4–6 feet (1.2–1.8 m). Medium to large spread. Good for medium to large ponds with water up to 4 feet (1.2 m) deep.

Nelumbo 'Baiyun Wanlian'

White with pale pink tips. Semidouble, very star-shaped blooms of up to 4 inches (10 cm). Height 2–3 feet (60–90 cm). Dwarf to small spread. Good for containers and small to medium ponds with water up to 6 inches (15 cm) deep.

Nelumbo 'Carolina Queen'

Deep pink with yellow centers. Single blooms of 8–12 inches (20–30 cm). Height 4–6 feet (1.2–1.8 m). Medium to large spread. Good for medium to large ponds with water up to 4 feet (1.8 m) or more deep.

Nelumbo 'Charles Thomas'

Lavender-pink. Single, fragrant blooms of 6–8 inches (15–20 cm). Height 3–4 feet (90–120 cm). Dwarf to small spread. Good for containers and small to medium ponds with water less than 2 feet (60 cm) deep.

Nelumbo 'Chawan Basu'

Pink edges that slowly mature through crystal white petals. Single blooms of 4–6 inches (10–15 cm). Height 2–3 feet (60–90 cm). Dwarf to medium spread. Good for containers and small to medium ponds with water less than 2 feet (60 cm) deep.

Nelumbo 'Chong Shui Hua'

Red-rose. Double blooms of up to 4 inches (10 cm). Height 2–3 feet (60–90 cm). Dwarf to small spread. Good for containers and small to medium ponds with water up to 6 inches (15 cm) deep.

Nelumbo 'Debbie Gibson'

Cream. Semidouble blooms of 6–10 inches (15–25 cm). Height 5–6 feet (1.5–1.8 m). Large spread. Good for medium to large ponds with water up to 4 feet (1.2 m) deep.

Nelumbo 'Double Pink'

Rose pink with pale centers. Double blooms of 6–8 inches (15–20 cm). Height 4–5 feet (1.2–1.5 m). Medium to large spread. Good for medium to large ponds with water to 2 or more feet (60 cm) deep.

Nelumbo 'Chong Shui Hua'

Nelumbo 'Double Pink'

Nelumbo 'Debbie Gibson'

Nelumbo 'Momo Botan'

Nelumbo 'Pekinensis Rubra'

Nelumbo 'Perry's Super Star'

Nelumbo 'Momo Botan'

Rosy pink. Double blooms of 4–6 inches (10–15 cm). Height 2–3 feet (60–90 cm). Small to medium spread. Good for containers and small to medium ponds with water up to 2 feet (60 cm) deep.

Nelumbo 'Pekinensis Rubra'

Deep rose-red. Single blooms of 8–12 inches (20–30 cm). Height 4–6 feet (1.2–1.8 m). Large spread. Good for medium to large ponds with water up to 6 feet (1.8 m) deep.

Nelumbo 'Perry's Super Star'

Pink and yellow-green. Semidouble blooms of 6–8 inches (15–20 cm). Height 3–5 feet (90–150 cm). Dwarf to medium spread. Good for small

Nelumbo 'Xiamen Bowl'

Nelumbo 'Shirokunshi'

Very snow white. Single blooms of 4–8 inches (10–20 cm). Height 2–3 feet (60–90 cm). Dwarf to medium spread. Good for containers and small to medium ponds with water less than 2 feet (60 cm) deep.

Nelumbo 'Xiamen Bowl'

Snow white and green. Single or semidouble blooms of up to 4 inches (10 cm). Height 2–3 feet (60–90 cm). Dwarf to small spread. Good for containers and small to medium ponds with water up to 6 inches (15 cm) deep. Synonym *Nelumbo* 'Rice Paper'.

Nelumbo 'Shirokunshi'

to large ponds with water up to 2 feet (60 cm) deep. This is Greg's favorite lotus. If you can have only one lotus, choose this one.

Marginal water plants grow and thrive at the edge, or margin, of the pond, where they soften the transition between rock and water, are often vital in maintaining proper water quality, and attract wildlife to the pond. They prefer to have their roots or their crown in water, but their foliage for the most part emerges above soil and water. Some marginals grow best only in soil that is wet but not submerged. Others prefer waterlogged soil and perhaps a slight amount of water over the top of their crown. Still others will thrive if their roots and growing crown are a few inches, or even a foot (30 cm) or more, below the water surface.

Marginals are not usually fussy or hard to maintain as long as their soil is roughly neutral in pH. Many will tolerate soils that are slightly acidic or slightly alkaline. A few, such as northern calla lily (*Calla palustris*) and pitcher plants (*Sarracenia*), require acidic soil and will languish if this condition is not met. Such particularity is rare and is noted, when necessary, in the plant descriptions that follow. Like all plants, marginals perform best when they are adequately fertilized during spring and summer. No other generalizations about growing conditions or seasonal care can be made about this very diverse group of plants.

Depending on their growth habits, marginals are planted in a variety of ways. Some grow from a central crown, others grow from underground rhizomes, and still others crawl across the soil surface. Most marginals grow perfectly well in plastic or mesh pots, but many are highly suitable for the bog garden, where they are freed from such restraints. If using a pot, be sensitive to the plant's natural growth habit. Following are the basic categories of growth habits for marginal plants and the corresponding ways to plant them.

Marginals with a Rhizome

The most commonly grown marginal in this group is sweet flag (*Acorus calamus*). It is potted the same way as water iris, by dividing the rhizome and placing it on the soil surface, and then covering the rhizome with only a slight amount of soil.

The closely related Japanese sweet flag (*Acorus gramineus*) produces a single fan-shaped stem. Its potting requirements fall somewhere between water iris and single-stemmed marginals (which see following). To make an effective planting, multiple fans need to be planted in one pot. Fill the pot two-thirds full of soil and place the rhizomes in the center of the pot. Face the fans outward in a roughly triangular fashion to allow them to branch and fill out the pot while forming a cluster in the center. Finally, fill the pot with soil, using enough to anchor the fans firmly in place.

Marginals with a Single Stem

Marginals that form a colony of individual stems include lizard tail (*Saururus cernuus*), *Lysimachia*, and water willow (*Justicia americana*). To grow these plants, fill the pot about two-thirds full with soil. Make a hole in the soil in the center of the pot, and place more than one stem in the hole. Move the soil back around the stems, adding more soil to fill the pot. These plants root from their stems, so their roots may be placed well below the soil surface.

Marginals with a Central Crown or Cluster of Stems

Umbrella grasses (*Cyperus*), sedges (*Carex*), and rushes (*Eleocharis*, *Juncus*, and *Scirpus*) branch from a central crown or cluster of stems. To grow these marginals, fill the pot two-thirds full with

Opposite: Marginal plants surround hardy waterlilies (center) and lotus (left foreground) in a canal.

soil. Place the plant in the center, spreading the roots around the pot. Then fill the pot with soil. Generally, the crown or rhizome can be covered with about 1 inch (2.5 cm) of soil to help it anchor into the soil. Do not submerge the pots for at least a week after they have been potted. Instead, keep the water at the crown level.

Marginals with a Single Crown

Examples of marginals that grow from a single crown or tuber include pickerel plant (*Pontederia*), water plantain (*Alisma*), lobelias, monkey flower (*Mimulus*), bog arum (*Peltandra virginica*), and gold club (*Orontium aquaticum*). To

Acorus calamus, catkin and foliage

grow these plants, simply fill the pot about two-thirds full of soil, place the plant in the center of the pot with the roots spread out over the soil, and cover the roots with soil. The crown of the plant, which is the "union" between the roots and stems, can usually be about 1 inch (2.5 cm) below the soil surface.

Marginals with a Running Stem

Pennywort (*Hydrocotyle*) and water clover (*Marsilea*) grow from roots that run across the top of the soil. To pot marginals with running stems, fill a pot with soil and top off with sand or pea gravel. Water the soil thoroughly. Put a hole in the center of the pot about 1-1/2–2 inches (4–5 cm) deep and insert 5 to 10 stem cuttings. Push the soil back around the stems, and submerge the pots in the pond.

ACORUS
Sweet flag

Sweet flags are an invaluable addition to the water garden for their neat, clean appearance. Hardy and foolproof, they add great textural interest to the pond. Taller forms provide an upright, architectural accent, and smaller selections have a graceful, arching appearance. The flowers are conelike and inconspicuous on the smaller forms. They are borne on hooklike clubs that appear in summertime about one-third to halfway up from the base of the foliage. These clubs turn brown when mature. On some selections, the clubs are very difficult to find and often go completely unnoticed.

All sweet flags grow well in sun to shade and require soil that is constantly moist. Underwatering causes the leaf tips to burn. Seasonal flooding does no harm, but the different species and cultivars vary in the amount of water they will tolerate over their crowns.

All sweet flags tolerate freezing temperatures and can freeze solid provided they remain in water while frozen. If they are removed from the water garden, they may be overwintered by mulching them into the perennial border. Care should be taken that they do not dry out during winter, or they will become parched and die.

Sweet flags are generally easy to grow and pest-free. Smaller forms are prone to spider mites. Larger selections may develop a fungus that causes black spots that can kill all the foliage. Clean up dead foliage in the fall, or as the black spots appear.

Acorus calamus/americana

A decorative, hardy pond plant that is sometimes mistaken for water iris because of its leaf shape, *Acorus calamus* is native to North America and can be found growing wild in marshy areas from Nova Scotia to Texas and westward to the Oregon coast. It grows from roots that run freely. Although it is not invasive, the plant's best ornamental value is achieved by keeping it in a pot, even in an earth-bottom pond. Leaves reach 3 feet (90 cm) high and fall off in winter. The plant tolerates water depths up to 6 inches (15 cm). Zones 4–11.

Acorus calamus 'Variegatus'

'Variegatus' (variegated sweet flag) has beautiful green-and-white foliage that blends well with the blue flowers of irises, blue pickerel plant (*Pontederia cordata*), and water forget-me-not (*Myosotis scorpioides*). Although it tolerates up to 6 inches (15 cm) of water over the crown, just moist soil is best. Leaves reach 2–3 feet (60–90 cm) high.

Acorus gramineus
Japanese sweet flag

Native to Japan, China, Korea, and Southeast Asia, this sweet flag is more restrained and will not run rampant throughout the pond as the larger sweet flag, *Acorus calamus*, is prone to do. Instead, Japanese sweet flag forms small clumps, like hosta. Plants are especially attractive at the edge of the pond or stream in only 1–2 inches (2.5–5 cm) of water, or in just damp soil. They reach 8–12 inches (20–30 cm) high and will spread 12 inches (30 cm) across. They are generally evergreen in colder climates. Zones 5–11.

'Golden Pheasant' is identical to the species but has all golden foliage in sun, chartreuse foliage in shade.

Acorus calamus, habit

Acorus gramineus

Acorus gramineus 'Licorice'

'**Licorice**' is identical to the species in size and habit but has darker green foliage that smells remarkably like licorice when bruised or crushed. Plant at a water depth of 1 inch and it will grow 1 foot (30 cm) high and wide.

'**Oborozuki**', a smaller selection with yellow-striped foliage, reaches about 8 inches (20 cm) in height and spread. It will grow well in moist soil or with up to 1 inch (2.5 cm) of water over its crown.

'**Ogon**' (golden Japanese sweet flag) has light green foliage accented with bright yellow stripes. It tolerates shade and is evergreen in many climates, generally Zone 6 and above. This cultivar is great for keeping color all winter in the water garden. Give it moist soil or up to 2 inches (5 cm) of water. It grows 8–12 inches (20–30 cm) high and spreads 12 inches (30 cm).

'**Pusillus**' is a dwarf form with dark green grasslike foliage, growing to only 4–5 inches (10–13 cm) tall and wide. It is ideal for the edge of the pond where people may tread, since it tolerates light foot traffic. Grow it in moist soil in sun to shade.

'**Pusillus Minimus**' (miniature Japanese sweet flag) is a rare form that grows to only about 2-1/2 inches (6 cm) tall and wide. It is sometimes used in bonsai but is nice as an evergreen pond edging. It does best in moist soil but can take up to 1/2 inch (12 mm) of standing water.

Acorus gramineus 'Ogon'

Acorus gramineus 'Pusillus Minimus Aurea'

Acorus gramineus
'Variegatus'

Acorus gramineus
'Yodo-no-yuki'

'Pusillus Minimus Aurea' (miniature golden Japanese sweet flag), another rare miniature form, is golden yellow and reaches only 2 inches (5 cm) tall and wide. It does best in just moist soil but can take water 1/2 inch (12 mm) deep.

'Variegatus' (variegated Japanese sweet flag), the white-striped cousin of 'Ogon', is excellent in the margin of the pond or in the perennial border. It is good for keeping winter color in the water garden in Zone 6 and up. Spreading to 12 inches (30 cm) and reaching a height of 8–10 inches (20–25 cm), it will take moist soil or up to 1 inch (2.5 cm) of water.

'Yodo-no-yuki' has green leaves streaked in yellow along the midrib. It reaches about 8 inches (20 cm) tall and wide and is sometimes confused with 'Ogon' in the trade. Plant at a water depth of 1 inch (2.5 cm).

Acrostichum danaeifolium

Acrostichum danaeifolium
Water leather fern

A true fern, *Acrostichum danaeifolium* is noted for its large fern-shaped leaves that take on a shiny, leathery texture. It makes a bold statement in larger ponds and is a wonderful accent plant. The leaves appear almost plastic and assume a cinnamon shade due to the great number of spores they produce on their undersides. Native to southern Florida, the species has two forms: an inland and a coastal. Both grow to enormous proportions under good conditions. After only a few months of the warm climate they prefer, plants we grew reached 9–11 feet (2.7–3.4 m) tall. Listed stature of these plants is 1–12 feet (30–360 cm) tall and wide. Recommended water depth is moist to 3 inches (7.5 cm), but mature plants can tolerate up to 18 inches (45 cm). If the water level is kept constant, the plant has a tendency to form a thick mound of rootstock. Plants do best in shade and can do quite well in interior waterscapes in relatively poor light. In full sun, the leaves take on a yellow cast. Zones 9–11.

Water leather fern will safely overwinter in a greenhouse where the water and air temperatures do not fall below 45°F (7°C). No special pruning is required. Cut back dead or dying leaves. The plant has no known pests.

ALISMA
Water plantain

Alisma is a genus of herbaceous perennials with spoon- or lance-shaped, deeply veined, somewhat spongy foliage. When plants are grown along the edge of a pond or stream, the leaves stand erect above the water. Though bearing a close resemblance to the leaves of melon sword (*Echinodorus*), these are more supple and pliable. When grown submerged, water plantain leaves become long and ribbonlike and are difficult to distinguish from submerged arrowhead (*Sagittaria*) or *Vallisneria*.

The flower heads, which appear in summer and continue through fall, are arranged in whorls that form large pyramid-shaped clouds of white, pink, or lavender. The flowers last long into the winter and provide a focal point that gives the pond depth and interest even during this otherwise drab time of year.

Water plantains are suitable for medium to large ponds. Situate them in sun to part shade and they will reach a height of 12–36 inches (30–90 cm) and a spread of 18 inches (45 cm). They self-seed freely if not deadheaded on a regular basis and can become well established in a short period of time in an earth-bottom pond. They generally prefer soil that is moist or up to 3 inches (7.5 cm) under water, though a few exceptions tolerate deeper water. They are not a pest in areas where water levels stay constant, but can become a nuisance in ponds or streams with fluctuating water levels.

All *Alisma* species may remain in the pond to freeze solid, provided they stay in the water. A period of winter chilling is essential to the plant's growth and flowering in subsequent seasons. Zones 3–11.

Alisma lanceolatum
Lance-leafed water plantain
Alisma lanceolatum has longer, narrower leaves than *A. plantago-aquatica*. The leaves are also slightly more blue-green and heavier textured, and the lavender flowers have a pink blush. When grown in 24 inches (60 cm) of water, the plant makes it to the surface and flowers. The species grows wild in Europe and into northern Africa and southern Asia.

Alisma plantago-aquatica
Water baby's breath
The most commonly available *Alisma*, this robust water plant flowers well. The tapered leaves are 4 inches (10 cm) wide and 6–8 inches (15–20 cm) long, and can be pure green to red-backed with red stems. The flowers are white to pink. The plant tolerates seasonal flooding and can be grown in water 12–24 inches (30–60 cm) deep. Native to the Northern Hemisphere, and in North America primarily in the eastern and midwestern regions, this species grows in marshy areas from Quebec east to Wisconsin and as far south as Alabama. Synonym *Alisma subcordatum*.

Alisma lanceolatum

Alisma plantago-aquatica

Alternanthera cardinalis

ALTERNANTHERA

Alternanthera is a genus of tropical marginals that provide cover and shade for fish in ponds, streams, and waterfalls. Low-growing, the plants often trail out on the water surface. They are also suitable for growing in hanging baskets. In the water garden, they clamber at the base of taller marginals, such as *Canna*, umbrella grass (*Cyperus*), or *Thalia*, weaving together larger plantings and hiding the edges of pots or stones. All the alternantheras grow equally well above or at the waterline. When grown submerged, they must have crystal clear water or will be prone to rot away and die. When grown as marginals in fully moist soil, they provide color and interest and are very carefree.

Alternantheras produce white flowers at any time. Most will grow to less than 6 inches (15 cm) high and will spread 12 inches (30 cm) or more. Native to tropical areas of South America, they are killed by frost. To overwinter plants, keep them in temperatures above 50°F (10°C) and supply extra light to make 12-hour days, so they will not flower themselves to death. Mealybugs, spider mites, and aphids can be a threat, especially in indoor environments, but simply submerging the plant in water for a day or two will take care of the problem Zones 9–11.

Alternanthera cardinalis
Cardinal leaf

Often found as an aquarium plant, this species is easily distinguished by its bright crimson leaf underside. Leaves are broader than in some of the other species and are often slightly ruffled at the edges. This species may grow slightly taller, up to 8 inches (20 cm), performing best when grown just at the water surface. *Alternanthera cardinalis* is native to southern Brazil.

Alternanthera philoxeroides
Alligator weed

Stems root at the edge of the pond and then float out onto the water surface, trailing sometimes up to 20 feet (6 m). The leaves are small, rounded, and fleshy. Flowers are small white powder puffs held on stalks near the base of the leaves. This species can become a nuisance in warmer climates and should be used with caution in areas where winters do not provide a killing frost. It grows in water up to 3 inches (7.5 cm) deep, or floating, and can also grow in drier soil. Crayfish farms often use this plant as a food source, and in the ornamental pond it is a great food for koi.

Alternanthera philoxeroides

Alternanthera reineckii

Alternanthera sessilis

Alternanthera reineckii
Copperleaf, ruby runner
Foliage is a distinctive purple-red, accented by white flowers that resemble blooms of clover. The plant has an open, trailing habit that makes it suitable for any size pond. Copperleaf is best grown as a marginal rather than a submerged water plant. It will tolerate deeper water for very short periods of time, but it has a tendency to let go of the soil if the water is deeper than 3 inches (7.5 cm). It will float to the surface and find a place to root at the water's edge. Situate it in sun to only part shade.

Alternanthera sessilis
Purple-leafed alternanthera
This species is yet another aquarium plant that easily adapts to the edge of the pond, or even to an annual planter alongside impatiens and petunias. The foliage color resembles the purple-red of copperleaf (*Alternanthera reineckii*), but its habit is more upright, rather than trailing along the water surface. It also differs from the other species by having narrower leaves and a bushier habit. It will grow to a height of 12–18 inches (30–45 cm).

Apios americana
Water wisteria, Indian potato
Brick-red to pinkish brown clusters of wisteria-like flowers emerge on vertical stems from summer to fall. Plants left to crawl along the ground rarely flower. Flower clusters are about 3–4 inches (7.5–10 cm) long and showiness varies greatly. Hairy, dull green, compound leaves having about five to nine leaflets also look just like those of wisteria. This plant comes in a great variety of colors and flower-cluster lengths, but no selections have been named.

Apios americana grows best in part shade but can tolerate sun. It generally climbs as high as 6 feet (1.8 m) or so, spreading only 1–3 feet (30–90 cm). After a few years, however, a wider colony will have developed. It grows in wet soil and survives seasonal flooding, but it needs water below the crown during the summer to do well. The species is native to eastern North

America. Often late in the year plants are infected by spider mites, much like soybeans are. The plants require no special care to overwinter but need to go dormant. They get weak if kept growing year-round. Zone 4 and up.

Arundo donax
Giant reed

Tall, stately, and highly ornamental, giant reed tolerates wide-ranging environments, including sandy soils to heavy clay, in alkaline or saline conditions. It often grows to 12 feet (3.6 m) tall in the pond. Plants resemble large corn stalks or sugar canes, with wide leaves that can be several inches long, tapering to a point. Flowers are large panicles of silver plumes 2 feet (60 cm) long that bloom in late summer or fall and quickly turn beige, remaining long into the winter. They are excellent cut flowers and dry well for long-lasting enjoyment indoors. The plants make an interesting winter accent in the pond and can be cut back once they become too tattered from wind and snow.

Giant reed grows best in full sun but can tolerate some shade. The soil can be dry or take a seasonal inundation of 1–3 inches (2.5–7.5 cm). The plant does best with more fertilizer in the spring than in the summer, allowing it to harden off by fall. In warmer climates it grows throughout the year and needs no period of winter dormancy. In colder areas where frost occurs, it turns brown and dies back to the ground. It is also extremely

Arundo donax

Apios americana

Arundo donax 'Variegata'

3–5 feet (90–150 cm). It grows in moist soil or up to 3 inches (7.5 cm) of water.

ASCLEPIAS
Milkweed, butterfly plant

Asclepias species are upright, cheerfully colored aquatics excellent for the edge of the pond. They attract many of the fluttering garden dwellers, especially monarch and viceroy butterflies. The pink, orange, yellow, or white flowers bloom in summer. Leaves are willowlike. Plants reach 1–3 feet (30–90 cm) tall and spread generally 1 foot (30 cm). Native to the Americas, milkweeds grow in sun to part shade in moist soil or wet meadows. They can stand some seasonal flooding as well. No special overwintering care is required where the species are hardy, but a dormant period is necessary. If bringing the plants indoors for the winter, keep them in a cool place. Zones 3–11, depending on species.

Asclepias curassavica
Blood flower

A tall plant for the wet edge, *Asclepias curassavica* grows 3 feet (90 cm) high and spreads just 6 inches (15 cm) in soil up to 1 inch (2.5 cm) under water. All summer long it bears orange-and-yellow or all-gold flowers in the leaf axils, not terminally like other forms of *Asclepias*. The species is native to Mexico and South America. Bring plants indoors before frost. Zone 10.

'Red Butterfly' produces red-and-yellow flowers.

'Silky Gold' bears golden yellow flowers.

Asclepias incarnata
Butterfly weed, swamp milkweed

Prized for its late-summer color, *Asclepias incarnata* can be used with other milkweeds in the perennial border, such as *A. tuberosa*, to link the pond visually with the rest of the landscape.

Asclepias incarnata will reach a height of 2–3 feet (60–90 cm) and can tolerate up to 5 inches (13 cm) of water. The narrow, willow-shaped foliage often turns color in the fall. Flowers are small, held in umbels at the top of each stem.

important to keep the crown of the plant cool during the winter. A freak warm spell can bring a plant out of dormancy, causing it to die once the colder weather inevitably returns. No pests have been noted. Zones 5–11.

'Golden Chain' has yellow leaves with green central stripes.

'Peppermint Stick' has bold green and white stripes that don't fade in heat or drought.

'Variegata' (variegated giant reed) has bold white and green leaves that create a striking bamboo effect. Shorter than the all-green species, it is more suitable for a smaller pond, reaching 3–8 feet (90–250 cm) tall with a spread of

Asclepias curassavica

Asclepias incarnata

They range in color from clear white to light pink to darker rose and even bitones. Seed heads have the characteristic half-moon shape and are filled with black seeds attached to strands of silk that float away on the air when the seed heads burst in early fall. The species is native to North America from Quebec to the Gulf of Mexico and westward to North Dakota, Wyoming, and New Mexico. It grows best if left in the pond during the winter. Zone 3.

'Ice Ballet' (white butterfly plant) has pure white flowers, which attract butterflies and hummingbirds, and make great cut flowers. Do not submerge the plant at the bottom of the pond.

Asclepias incarnata 'Ice Ballet'

Asclepias perennis

Asclepias rubra

Bacopa caroliniana

Asclepias perennis
Aquatic milkweed

Aquatic milkweed is a small, compact, bushy plant with fine willowy leaves and gleaming white to pale rose flowers. Reaching 1–2 feet (30–60 cm) tall, this native from the Carolinas to Texas grows in sun to shade and requires very moist soil or up to 6 inches (15 cm) of water. Zones 6–11.

Asclepias rubra

With rose to red flowers on bushy plants and willowlike leaves, *Asclepias rubra* is slightly shorter than *A. incarnata* and has smaller leaves. It grows to 2 feet (60 cm) high and is best in just moist soil but can take seasonal flooding. The species is native to coastal plains of New Jersey, Florida, and Texas. Zone (5)6.

BACOPA
Water hyssop

The low-growing tropical marginals in this genus are excellent as ground covers in the bog garden or near the edge of the pond, or as trailing plants in the waterfall or table-top pond. Native to the Americas, *Bacopa* species are dainty additions to any size of water feature and will even grow submerged under several inches of neutral to acidic water.

Foliage is usually small, rounded, and fleshy and often fragrant when crushed. Flowers bloom in summer. The plant creeps through sun or shade, generally reaching 2–4 inches (5–10 cm) high and spreading 24 inches (60 cm) in a season. It needs moist soil or water up to 1 inch deep. If cucumber beetles appear on emerged plants, simply submerge the plants for two to four days to eliminate the pests.

Bacopa grows year-round in warmer climates where frost is not an issue. In colder areas, cut about 3 inches (7.5 cm) from several tips of the plant and bring these tip cuttings indoors for the winter. Simply place them in a cup of water and keep them in a warm, sunny room of the house. They will root and grow during the winter and can be replanted in a pot and placed outdoors when the last chance of freezing has passed.

Bacopa caroliniana
Lemon bacopa, lemon water hyssop

An easy-to-grow ground cover for the water garden, lemon bacopa is a good addition to the container water garden on the patio, where its heavily lemon-scented foliage and bright blue flowers can be enjoyed all summer long. It is also a good choice for a flooded meadow or storm water detention area, since it will grow fully submerged. Streams and bogs are great environments, too. The species is native to the coastal plain from Virginia to Florida to Texas. Zones 9–11.

Bacopa monnieri
Water purslane

Water purslane is a perfect, creeping ground cover with small light green leaves and nearly ever-blooming white flowers striped pink, lavender, or blue. It can take light foot traffic and would be useful in water detention basins where it can be mowed. It is very adaptable and more tolerant of seasonal water fluctuations than other bacopas. It can grow submerged in several inches of clear, neutral to acidic water, and typically grows in meadows flooded with water 4–12 inches (10–30 cm) deep. It reaches up and out of the water, hiding the surface. The species is native to coastal Virginia, south to Florida, and west to Texas and throughout tropical South America. Zones 6–11.

Baldellia ranunculoides f. repens
Siberian pink cup

Siberian pink cup has dense clouds of 1/2-inch (12-mm) pink flowers with yellow centers that resemble poppies. The delicate blossoms adorn tufts of foliage 2–10 inches (5–25 cm) high and 10–12 inches (25–30 cm) wide all summer long, lending an airy look to the water garden. The plant is excellent for a tub garden, along the pool edge, or in a stream under sun to part shade. Give it moist soil or water up to 1/2 inch (12 mm) deep. It will also grow submerged in clear water but will not flower.

Bacopa monnieri

Baldellia ranunculoides f. repens

Native to Europe and northern Africa, *Baldellia ranunculoides* f. *repens* is hardy in Zones 6–11, but it needs some shade to survive south of Zone 8 or the heat will kill it. It needs no special care to overwinter in Zones 6–9, where it will go dormant naturally, but in harsher climates it can be brought in and overwintered in a sunny window or under lights. If not given additional light in the winter, short days of less than 10 hours of sunlight will send it into senescence and you may lose it. Aphids may appear on the plants.

Baumea rubiginosa 'Variegata'

Baumea rubiginosa 'Variegata'
Golden spears, variegated water chestnut

This fine plant has tubular leaves that are flat like a fencing foil. Colored dark green, they are marked with a yellow vertical line that remains stable throughout the growing season. Flowers are small brown tassels that appear in the fall. The plant has a running habit and reaches a height of 1–2 feet (30–60 cm). It prefers moist soil or water up to 2 inches (5 cm) over the crown and will tolerate seasonal flooding of 10 inches (25 cm) or more. Situate it in sun to part shade. Plants will overwinter outdoors as long as their roots remain below the freezing line. In very cold areas that can reach down to -20°F (-29°C), store the plant in a cooler where it will remain damp but will be protected from freezing. A black spot problem can develop, but it tends to disappear with fertilizing. Also, grasshoppers have been known to chew up the plant. The species is native to Madagascar, Indonesia, Australia, and Tasmania. Zones 6b–11.

Butomus umbellatus
Flowering rush

This delicate beauty displays large umbels of white to pink flowers all summer and onionlike foliage. It is an excellent companion of tall rushes (*Scirpus*, *Schoenoplectus*) and cattails (*Typha*). Flowering rush needs sun to part shade and moist soil or water to 1 inch deep. It tolerates seasonal flooding and can take sustained deeper water, up to 4 inches (10 cm), in the summer, but it flowers more in shallower water. Plants generally reach 1–3 feet (30–90 cm) high and 14 inches (35 cm) wide. This species has been listed as an invasive in some areas.

With a native range from Europe and across Russia to the Pacific Ocean, the species is very hardy and needs no special care over winter but must have a period of dormancy. In warmer climates place it in the fridge for about 60 days. Grasshoppers and woolly caterpillars are the only known pests. Earned Royal Horticultural Society Award of Garden Merit in 1993. Zones 3–11.

Butomus umbellatus

Butomus umbellatus f. *juncus* in a wetland planting

Calla palustris

Forma junceus is taller than the species and more upright with larger flower heads. It is very rushy looking, with twisted leaves growing in fans. The leaves often turn brown as the plant ages.

'**Rosenrot**' has pink flowers.

'**Schneeweisschen**' has white flowers. Its stems and leaves lack the characteristic blue blush of the species.

Calla palustris
Northern calla lily

This cold-loving aquatic has glossy, heart-shaped leaves on floating stems accented in spring by 2-inch (5-cm) white flowers. It requires highly acidic water and soil. In its native habitat in Europe, Asia, and North America, it floats out into part or full shade on mats of dead oak and pine foliage. In the fall, it decorates the pond with its seed heads of bright red berries. It reaches only about 4 inches (10 cm) high but has a running

Caltha natans

spread. It overwinters easily when its rhizomes are left in the water. Zones 2–6.

Grow northern calla lily in moist soil or give it free rein to float. It may be bothered by a caterpillar that bores into the stems, but it is occasional and rarely fatal.

CALTHA
Marsh marigold, elkslip

Caltha is much favored by water gardeners for its early spring flowers that open bright yellow or white long before the rest of the pond has come back to life. The round, usually kidney-shaped leaves are dark green, glossy, and toothed around the edges. The flowers have five to nine sepals (no petals) and are usually single. Plants have a round, mounded habit and grow in clumps, similar to hostas.

Calthas generally grow in moist to wet, boggy conditions along the edges of creeks, streams, and ponds. They can often be found growing naturally in wet swales, especially under the canopy of tall deciduous trees. In cooler climates they grow from spring through fall, while in warmer areas they may die back to the ground during the strong heat and humidity of summer.

Most calthas are best cultivated in moist soil or water up to 1 inch (2.5 cm) deep under sun or part shade. All like cool weather and do poorly in areas of high summer heat and humidity. They do best in areas with cool nights. Calthas prefer to overwinter in cooler conditions and require a period of cold dormancy to bloom well the following season. Aphids may be a pest.

Caltha natans
Floating marsh marigold

Growing underwater much like a waterlily with floating leaves and submerged stems, this species has a small white flower in early spring that floats on the water surface. It is particularly

Caltha palustris

Caltha palustris
'Semiplena'

sensitive to warmer temperatures and fades, and then dies, if not kept in cool, running water. It is native to Alaska and southward into northern Minnesota. Zones 3–5. Grow this in part shade at a water depth of 4–6 inches (10–15 cm), giving it slightly acidic soil. It grows 2 inches (5 cm) above the water—enough for just the flower really—and spreads 12 inches (30 cm). In addition to the aphids attracted to most calthas, China mark moth may appear on this species.

Caltha palustris
Cowslip, marsh marigold
This harbinger of spring is one of the first marginals to bloom, awakening the pond with bright and cheerful yellow flowers. Leaves are dark green and glossy, resembling those of violets, and usually toothed at the edges. The plant may rebloom in areas with cool summers, but in areas of hot summers, the leaves sometimes die back. Its native range is circumboreal as far south as Tennessee. Zones 3–7. Cowslip grows to 12 inches (30 cm) tall and spreads 12–18 inches (30–45 cm). It tolerates seasonal flooding. Some selections grow in up to 6 inches (15 cm) of water. Earned Royal Horticultural Society Award of Garden Merit in 1993. Although it may be hard to find some of these selections, they are well worth the effort.

'Alba', small white flowers.

'Auenwald', large yellow-gold flowers.

'Flore Pleno', double yellow flowers with full-sized petals. Earned Royal Horticultural Society Award of Garden Merit in 1993.

'Goldshale', green-gold flowers.

Var. himalensis, red to orange flowers with red to yellow stamens.

'Honeydew', green-yellow flowers with very large petals.

'Marilyn', masses of canary yellow flowers.

'Multiplex', double orange-yellow flowers with smaller petals, like a little mum.

'Plena', double yellow flowers with full-sized petals.

Var. radicans produces new plants on flower stems.

'Semiplena', lemon yellow flowers with a double row of full-sized petals.

'Stagnalis', very upright foliage, grayish green-yellow flowers.

'Susan', many large lemon yellow flowers per stem.

'Tyermannii', dark purple stems, yellow flowers.

CANNA
Tall and impressive, cannas are topped by extremely colorful flowers that start in midsummer and keep going until frost. Two kinds of cannas are suitable for the water garden. The true water cannas grow well in saturated soil or with water over their crowns and bloom throughout the summer. The water-tolerant cannas are terrestrial forms that grow in the perennial border but can also adapt to growing in waterlogged soil. Some usually terrestrial cannas that flower just in late summer will bloom all season when grown in water.

Cannas commonly grow to several feet high in a single season, forming a large mass of tubers at the base. They are suitable as accent plants in the water garden and make excellent specimens when planted in a container. Lower growing, more creeping water plants, such as *Bacopa* or *Hydrocotyle*, are good understory complements to the large, bold effect of a canna.

Canna foliage is large, long, and tapered—very tropical looking. Hues range from bright green to blue-green, dark purple, or crimson. Some leaves are striped in yellow, white, or red. Flowers also come in a wide variety of colors, from delicate creams and yellows to brassy oranges and reds. They are either gladiola-type, with large overlapping petals, or plumeria-type, with a more delicate, narrow form.

Full sun is best for bringing out the strongest color and most flowers, but cannas will grow in pretty deep shade. They reach 2–9 feet (60–270 cm) tall and 2–6 feet (60–180 cm) wide. All take moist soil or water over their crowns to varying depths, up to 12 inches (30 cm) depending on the species or cultivar. Zones 8b–11.

It is usually recommended that cannas be brought indoors for the winter. They can also be left to dry out, so the tubers can be cleaned and stored for the winter. Robert Armstrong, who hybridized the famed Longwood water cannas, successfully overwinters his hybrids in his Pennsylvania garden by cutting them back and placing them at the bottom of the pond. As long as the rhizomes are not reached by ice during the winter, the plants return the following spring.

Not prone to severe attacks by pests, cannas may be affected by aphids or Japanese beetles during the summer. If brought indoors to grow during the winter, they may develop spider mites. Canna rust may also occur among plants

Canna 'Endeavor'

Canna 'Durban'

Canna 'Erebus'

that are not kept very wet or are not cleaned well in the fall before being put away for the winter. Rust looks like orange pustules, or iron rust, on the leaves. It usually begins on the lower leaves and progresses up the plant as the infection spreads. Just cut back affected foliage and destroy. Clean tools and wash hands between plants. Sanitation is the best cure for canna rust.

Canna 'Durban'

Bright tomato red flowers sit well above foliage that is flushed in red and streaked with gold. This water-tolerant canna, sold as a water canna, needs moist to just wet soil. Height 5–8 feet (160–250 cm), spread 3–4 feet (90–120 cm).

Canna 'Endeavor'
Red water canna

This true water canna is distinguished by bold, red, butterfly-like flowers. It has blue-green foliage with a thin red edge and stems with a red blush at the base. It grows best in moist soil or in water up to 6 inches (15 cm) deep. Although it will tolerate deeper water, it will not thrive and flowering will be poor. 'Endeavor' is a hybrid between a red garden canna and *Canna glauca*. Aside from the color and slightly larger seeds, it can pass for *C. glauca* and is often sold as such. Height 4–5 feet (120–150 cm), spread 2–3 feet (60–90 cm).

Canna 'Erebus'
Peach water canna

The soft, delicate, pinky peach blooms of this true water canna are a rare color for the water garden. Plants thrive in moist soil or water up to 10 inches (25 cm) deep. Earned Royal Horticulture Society Award of Garden Merit in 2002. Height 2–6 feet (60–180 cm), spread 2–3 feet (60–90 cm).

Canna 'Florence Vaughn'
Orange-yellow water canna

Probably the most water tolerant of the non-aquatic cannas, 'Florence Vaughn' takes as

much as 10 inches (25 cm) of water over its crown. The stunning flowers resemble giant pansies of orange edged in yellow. The plant is a real showstopper. Foliage is flat and green. Height 4–6 feet (120–180 cm), spread 2–3 feet (60–90 cm).

Canna 'Florence Vaughn'

Canna 'Intrigue' with darker-leaved, deeper red-flowered *C.* 'Black Knight'

Canna 'Panache'

Canna 'Phasion'

Canna 'Intrigue'
Purple water canna

This water-tolerant canna is often sold as a water canna. It fills a special niche among cannas with dark purple foliage and pink-orange flowers. It prefers moist soil, but will grow in as much as 10 inches (25 cm) of water. Height 6–10 feet (180–300 cm), spread 3–4 feet (90–120 cm).

Canna 'Panache'

A much sought after water-tolerant canna, 'Panache' has creamy plumeria-type flowers with raspberry red throats. It needs just moist soil and seems

not to be bothered by the usual pests. Height 5–6 feet (150–180 cm), spread 3–4 feet (90–120 cm).

Canna 'Phasion'

Many people try to use this water-tolerant canna as a water canna. It works under only moist to wet conditions with no depth of water. Also sold under the trademarked name Tropicanna, this selection has orange flowers. Leaves are heavily flushed in red and streaked with gold. Earned Royal Horticultural Society Award of Garden Merit in 2002. Height 5–8 feet (150–250 cm), spread 3–4 feet (90–120 cm).

Canna 'Pretoria'

Canna 'Pretoria'
Variegated water canna

A water-tolerant canna long sold as a water canna, 'Pretoria' has boldly striped banana-like foliage topped with large orange flowers streaked red. The effect is very exotic. The plant prefers moist soil but will grow well in up to 4 inches (10 cm) of water and will tolerate as much as 10 inches (25 cm). Height 4–6 feet (120–180 cm), spread 2–3 feet (60–90 cm).

Canna 'Ra'
Yellow water canna

'Ra' has strong canary yellow flowers and blue-green foliage. It is the tallest of the water cannas. Give it moist soil or water up to 10 inches (25 cm) deep. Earned Royal Horticultural So-ciety Award of Garden Merit in 2002. Height 4–6 feet (120–180 cm), spread 2–3 feet (60–90 cm).

Canna 'Striped Beauty'

This water-tolerant canna can grow in water up to 1 inch deep. Flowers are gladiola-type with white-and-yellow petals and red stems. Leaves are bright green striped in white. Synonym *Canna* 'Bengal Tiger'. Height 3–5 feet (90–150 cm), spread 3–4 feet (90–120 cm).

Canna 'Ra'

Canna 'Striped Beauty'

Canna 'Stuttgart'

Especially prized among canna collectors, this selection has flowers that open pale yellow and mature to a passion-fruit orange. Leaves are heavily streaked in white. The plant can be difficult in the landscape, however, because the leaves burn easily, making the plant look damaged. Grow it in moist soil or water up to 1 inch deep. The plant produces many green shoots without variegation, which should be removed. This canna tends not to be bothered by pests. Height 7–8 feet (210–250 cm), spread 3–4 feet (90–120 cm).

Canna 'Taney'
Orange water canna

A bright orange flower makes this water canna a particularly welcome addition to the pond. Give it moist soil or water up to 6 inches (15 cm) deep. Height 3–4 feet (90–120 cm), spread 1–2 feet (30–60 cm).

CAREX
Sedge

Carex is a genus of grasslike plants forming mounded tufts of foliage that are highly ornamental in the pond and water garden, along a stream or waterfall, or even in a container planting. Several species are truly aquatic. Many others are water tolerant or at least prefer evenly moist soil to grow well. Leaves are commonly triangular, V-, or M-shaped, with a distinctive midrib. They rise from a clump and often arch upward and outward. Flowers are not remarkable, being brown or green spikes that on certain species can only be found with some investigation.

Sedge colonies are common in bogs and fens, in wetland forests, and along the edges of lakes and ponds. They are an important part of the wetland ecology, serving as a kind of buffer zone. They fill in gradually as the shoreline recedes, replacing plants such as pickerel plant (*Pontederia*) and cattail (*Typha*) that grew there when the waters were deeper. Sedges can be difficult to distinguish from grasses, and even more difficult to distinguish from each other. They are found in many parts of the world,

Canna 'Stuttgart'

Canna 'Taney'

ranging from the tropics to more temperate climates. More than 500 species of *Carex* are native to North America alone. These are hiding spots for many insects and animals, especially frogs and other small water-loving amphibians. Those growing in shallow water provide spawning ground for fish. Sandhill cranes may be seen making their nests in the hills of a sedge meadow.

Sedges grow in sun to part shade in a wide range of pH levels and require no special care to overwinter in their hardiness zones. Mice, grasshoppers, and voles can be a problem. Especially in winter, mice and voles can destroy a stand of sedge by feasting on the shoots and roots.

Carex elata 'Aurea'
Golden variegated sedge

This golden cultivar is striking in the pond. It has bright yellow leaves accented by thin green lines. Color is better when the plant is grown in full sun, but it can tolerate shade. Flowers are brown spikes in summer. Grow this sedge in moist soil or water to 2 inches (5 cm) deep. It does best if the water is high in spring, then gradually receding in summer to keep the soil just wet. Height 24–36 inches (60–90 cm), spread 18 inches (45 cm). Zones 5–11. Synonym *Carex elata* 'Bowles' Golden'. Earned Royal Horticultural Society Award of Garden Merit in 1993.

Carex flacca
Blue sedge

The glowing, baby blue foliage of this European native is a worthy addition to the shade garden, although the plant also grows well in full sun. It is a perfect companion to hostas in the damp, shaded bog garden. It needs moist soil or water to 1 inch deep. Height 6–12 inches (15–30 cm), spread 6–12 inches (15–30 cm). Zones 5–11, with evergreen foliage. Brown flowers appear in spring.

Carex flacca

Carex flacca 'Bias'

Carex elata 'Aurea'

Carex muskingumensis 'Little Midge' and 'Oehme'

Carex pendula

'**Bias**' (variegated blue sedge) has a white margin along one edge of the leaf, sometimes both edges. The cool blue-and-white look lights up the darkest corner of the bog garden or pond.

Carex muskingumensis
Palm sedge

A native of the eastern United States, palm sedge looks like a bushy umbrella grass (*Cyperus*) or perhaps a dwarf water bamboo on steroids (*Dulichium arundinaceum*). It is often used in wetland reclamations. Easy to grow, it forms a clump much like a hosta and tolerates full shade, yet also grows in full sun, where it will take on a gold-green cast. The green to tan flowers bloom in early summer and are borne on the ends of the stalks. Height 12–18 inches (30–45 cm), spread 12 inches (30 cm). The plant does well in moist soil or water to 2 inches (5 cm) deep. Do not place it at the bottom of the pond to overwinter; it will not survive. Zones 4–9.

'**Ice Fountains**' has white-streaked foliage in the spring or in areas of cool nights.

'**Little Midge**' is a wonderful selection just 3–4 inches (7.5–20 cm) tall. This cute little sedge looks almost like pine moss or little pine trees. It is great as a ground cover or in a small dish garden.

'**Oehme**' has evenly green leaves in spring that become yellow-margined in summer and look almost gilded.

'**Silberstreif**' (silver stripe) has white margins on its leaves and grows slightly smaller than the species. It is similar to and may be the same as 'Ice Fountains'.

'**Wachtposten**' (sentry tower) is a large, more upright form with evenly dark green foliage.

Carex pendula
Drooping sedge

Long brown flower spikes dangle like earrings from tall, arching stems that reach 3–6 feet (90–180 cm) high. The plant forms neat clumps 4–5 feet (120–150 cm) wide and self-sows freely in the moderately warm climate it prefers. It is native to Eurasia and northern Africa. Where it is not hardy, bring it indoors to a sunny window in winter. It does well in moist soil or water to 4 inches (10 cm) deep. It is a favorite of grasshoppers. Zones (5)6–11.

'Cool Jazz' offers cool green leaves with a cream strip down the center that lasts all summer.

'Moonraker' has heavily variegated foliage that is mostly cream-yellow with a green streak, especially in the spring. In some climates the variegation tends to fade in the summer and becomes lime green. Friends in the northwestern United States report that it is a great hit, not fading in summer.

Cephalanthus occidentalis
Button bush
This aquatic woody ornamental is an unusual specimen, truly a shrub rather than a perennial. Each summer it bursts into flower with white globes that look like fluffy, round cotton balls. In the fall, the whole bush turns crimson. No cultivars have been formally named, but some very nice red-tipped forms are available, with red petioles and glossy foliage. The species is native to eastern North America. Grow it in sun to part shade in moist soil or water to 18 inches (45 cm)

deep. It has no known pests. Height 3–6 feet (90–180 cm) high and 6–8 feet (180–250 cm) wide. Zones 3–10.

COLOCASIA
Elephant ears, taro
Bold and large-leafed, *Colocasia* is a genus of tender water plants that love lots of fertilizer and hot, humid weather. They make dramatic accent plants in the pond. They are ideal for container gardens as well as full-sized ponds because of their eye-catching foliage and graceful habit.

Native to tropical Asia, *Colocasia* species have naturalized throughout most tropical regions of the world. More than 300 varieties are grown in the United States, especially in Hawaii, many as a food crop. For the water garden, interest is more in the colorful leaf and petiole, the leaf stalk, of the cultivars. More often than not it is the petiole that comes in so many beautiful colors, and not the leaf. Concentrate on siting the plant to see "into" it to view the petioles. The petiole colors range from purple-black to creamy honeydew-white, with pink, red, striped, streaked, and smoky colors in between. This plant gives the garden designer a whole palette of colors.

Cephalanthus occidentalis

Taros may be overwintered in colder climates by bringing them indoors and keeping the pot in a saucer of water in a warm, sunny room. They may also be dried down to a tuber, which can be stored in coarse vermiculite in a sealed container. The plants will also overwinter if they are simply dried down in their pots and left in a cool but frost-free, dark spot where they will remain dormant until brought out again in the spring.

Taros are attractive to quite a number of pests: spider mites, mealybugs, Japanese beetles, and occasionally aphids. In Hawaii, they may also be affected by pink root aphids. They seem susceptible to the incurable Dasheen mosaic virus as well.

Colocasia esculenta
Green taro

Green taro makes a good backdrop for more delicate plants. Green to pale yellow flowers bloom in summer on a plant that reaches 2–6 feet (60–180 cm) high and spreads 2–4 feet (60–120 cm). Grow it in sun to part shade in moist soil or water to 6 inches (15 cm) deep. Zones 9–11. Earned Royal Horticultural Society Award of Garden Merit in 1993.

'Akado' grows to more than 3 feet (90 cm) tall and displays coffee-colored stems.

'Black Magic' (sometimes sold as 'Jet Black Wonder') has leaves and petioles that are very dark, almost black-purple.

'Bun Long' grows to 3 feet (90 cm) tall and has distinct crinkly, cupped, green foliage that faces upward. It gives a great, unusual texture to the water garden.

'Eleele Naioea' grows to only 2 feet (60 cm) high and shows black petioles.

'Elepaio' has the striking look of leaves splattered with white paint. At times leaves are completely white, at other times they are barely touched. Leaves are large given the plant's shorter, 2-foot (60-cm) stature.

'Matale' sports bright strawberry red petioles against large green leaves edged in red.

Colocasia esculenta 'Black Magic'

Colocasia esculenta 'Metallica'

'Metallica' (violet-stemmed taro) is a particularly elegant cultivar with deep purple petioles and large, velvety, blue-green leaves.

'Nancy's Revenge' is known for a prominent white blotch in the center of the leaf.

'Purple Manalud' offers giant cranberry-colored petioles and big blue-green leaves with a red edge. Even the backs of the leaves have cranberry veins. The plant grows to 4-1/2 feet (1.3 m) tall.

'Ualtia Pele' (sometimes sold as 'Kanapaha' or 'Black Marble') is blue-green overlaid with purple smoke and flecks. Light purple petioles are streaked in dark purple. The plant makes a perfect accent next to yellows and whites. It grows to more than 3 feet (90 cm) tall.

Cotula coronopifolia

Colocasia jensii
Black princess taro

Slightly shorter than some other taros, this species has bright green leaves with blue-purple blushing between the veining. Petioles are green. The effect is subtle and very pleasing. The plant has a clumping habit and in summer produces green flowers blushed with blue-purple. It grows 2–4 feet (60–120 cm) tall and wide. Site it in sun to part shade in moist soil or water to 6 inches (15 cm) deep. Zones 9–11.

Cotula coronopifolia
Golden buttons

Accenting the fleshy foliage in summer are bright yellow buttons of flowers reminiscent of daisies. This marginal is delightful in the waterfall, at the pond's edge, or in a container water garden. A little shade, especially in the afternoon, helps to keep its bright green color and prevents it from wilting due to high heat and humidity. Height 10 inches (25 cm), spread 12 inches (30 cm). Native to South Africa. Grow in moist soil or water to 1 inch (2.5 cm) deep. Zones 6–8.

Golden buttons are generally easy to grow and are sometimes listed as invasive. We have found that ornamental fish nibble on their stems and prevent them from taking over the pond. They also are attractive to mealybugs if not well fed and growing like mad.

Colocasia jensii

CRINUM
Bog lily

More than 130 species of *Crinum* live in tropical regions around the world. The plants are noted for their large flowers composed of six long petals that droop or hang from the center of the blossom. Appearing in summer or early fall, they are very fragrant and look like starbursts. Color ranges from white to deep rose. Foliage is straplike and leathery, similar to *Amaryllis*, which is a distant relative. Zones 7–11.

The plant tolerates seasonal flooding, but does best in moist soil or water to 2 inches (5 cm) deep. It will grow through the fall and winter in warm, tropical climates. In colder areas, it should be brought indoors and overwintered much like a houseplant. Watch for spider mites and mealybugs at this time.

Crinum americanum
Water spider lily, swamp lily

This is the most commonly available species of *Crinum* in North America. It grows wild from Florida southward into Mexico and through

Crinum americanum

Central America into tropical South America. Flowers are usually white, although they may take on a pink blush, and as much as 4 inches (10 cm) in diameter. They appear in summer or fall. The plant grows in sun to only part shade and reaches 12–36 inches (30–90 cm) high and 12–48 inches (30–120 cm) wide. It does best in very wet soil or slightly under the water level.

Crinum erubescens 'West Indies'
Rastafari crinum

Rastafari crinum comes from the West Indies and has small white flowers that bloom in summer and little straplike foliage like large *Liriope*. It makes a great ground cover, growing to just 10 inches (25 cm) high and spreading 12 inches (30 cm). Grow it in sun to part shade in moist soil or water to 4 inches (10 cm) deep. Zones 9–11. The plant does not seem to be bothered by pests.

Cypella aquatica
Water tulip, water orchid

This elegant plant has intense yellow flowers that resemble open tulips or Chinese lanterns. It blooms in late spring to early summer. Leaves are heart-shaped and resemble palm foliage. Native to southern Brazil and northern Argentina, this plant reaches 12–36 inches (30–90 cm) tall and wide. Grow it from bulbs in moist soil or water to 2 inches (5 cm) deep in sun to part shade. Bring it indoors for the winter, or dry down bulbs to be stored like cannas or tropical waterlilies. Sometimes spider mites bother the plant. Zones 9–11.

CYPERUS

Cyperus species are mostly tropical water plants grown for their ornamental sprays of leaf fronds that resemble thin, papery palms. The large heads are held high atop triangular stems that sprout from a central clump. The "flowers" are really the seed heads, generally small and green, turning tawny brown as the seeds develop, usually on display in the summer. The overall appearance of the seed heads is unique to each species.

In ancient days, *Cyperus* foliage, especially from *C. papyrus*, was used to make paper products and to weave mats. Today the plants are useful and attractive accents in the water landscape. Larger specimens are stunning as a central focal point in the waterlily pond. Mixed with other large, tropical water plants, they make the bold statement of tropicalismo possible even in the water garden.

The plants provide shade at the edge of the pond and give some relief to shorter plants that benefit from being protected from the sun. All *Cyperus* species are heavy feeders and should be fertilized at least once a month. Besides their ornamental value, they are also excellent for pond filtration.

The tropical species overwinter easily in the sunny house or a greenhouse and are suitable as houseplants. They are occasionally bothered by mealybugs when brought indoors in winter.

Cyperus alternifolius
Umbrella grass

This species name and its synonym (*Cyperus involucratus*) are so mixed up in the water garden trade that controversy still surrounds them. *Cyperus alternifolius* is the standard umbrella grass most commonly sold to hobby pond keepers. It is popular for its easy nature and relaxed habit. At 4–6 feet (1.2–1.8 m) high, it sports a top sprout of leaves that can grow up to 2 feet (60 cm) across in mature specimens, forming the characteristic umbrella shape for which the plant is named. Individual leaves are generally narrow, about 1/2 inch wide (12 mm), but grow to 12 inches (30 cm) or more in length. The plant retains its clean, green color all year long in the warm climate it prefers.

It needs little care other than regular feeding during the spring and summer, and the occasional trimming of any brown leaf tips. Situate this plant in sun to part shade in moist soil or water to 6 inches (15 cm) deep or more. A native of Madagascar, the species will tolerate light frosts but not prolonged cold weather. The crown must never be allowed to freeze. In colder

Crinum erubescens 'West Indies'

Cypella aquatica

Cyperus alternifolius 'Denver Giant'

Cyperus alternifolius

climates, bring in tops and float them in water, or bring plants indoors, placing pots in a cat-litter tray of water in a sunny, frost-free location. Zones 7–11.

'**Denver Giant**' comes from a butterfly garden in Denver where Greg first saw it growing. Frond heads were 2 feet (60 cm) across and stood 8–9 feet (2.5–2.7 m) tall—truly an enormous plant for really large-scale settings. It has not attained that height in Greg's garden, but it is definitely larger than other selections.

'**Gracilis**' (miniature umbrella grass) has very narrow leaves that give the head a very fine-cut appearance. Refined and elegant, it is well suited to smaller water gardens and table-top ponds, or as a companion plant to bonsai. It grows 12 inches (30 cm) tall the first season and 24 inches (60 cm) the next, but its spread is rather narrow at 12 inches (30 cm). Give it moist soil or water to 4 inches (10 cm) deep. Synonym *Cyperus alternifolius* 'Strictus'.

'**Nanus**' (dwarf umbrella grass) is a compact plant with long umbrella fronds. Although it is shorter than the species, it is taller and lankier than 'Gracilis'. It grows 2–4 feet (60–120 cm) tall and wide.

'**Variegatus**' (variegated umbrella grass) offers an even more striking accent in the pond. A compact plant at 2 feet (60 cm) high and wide, it has irregular white stripes on long umbrella fronds. It reverts regularly and for no known reason; often all-green plants become variegated again. This selection is beautiful at its peak but difficult to keep there.

Cyperus giganteus
Mexican papyrus

A favorite of many water gardeners, Mexican papyrus has 20-inch (50-cm) spheres of wiry foliage on stiff, very erect, non-arching stems. The overall effect resembles balls of stars. The leaves are flat rather than the round strands of standard *Cyperus papyrus*. Grow it in sun to part shade in moist soil or water to 6 inches (15 cm) deep. Native to Mexico and south to South America, this species reaches 5–12 feet (1.5–3.6 m) tall and spreads 4–5 feet (1.2–1.5 m). To overwinter it, bring it indoors to a bright spot and keep well-watered or even place the pot in a shallow tray of water. Keep temperatures above 50°F (10°C). Zones 8–11.

Cyperus longus
Hardy umbrella grass, sweet galingale

This plant is not as showy as its tropical relatives. The frond heads have only five leaves or so, instead of the dozen or more that are common on other forms of *Cyperus*. Also, the leaves stand more upright, rather than hanging outward at a right angle from the main stem. Unlike other *Cyperus* species, this one has a running habit. It is striking in large patches, growing 2–4 feet (60–120 cm) high. The plant prefers acidic soil

Cyperus giganteus

Cyperus alternifolius 'Gracilis'

Cyperus alternifolius 'Nanus'

Cyperus longus

Cyperus prolifer

with a pH slightly over 8.5; closer to neutral produces better plants. It takes sun to part shade and moist soil or water to 6 inches (15 cm) deep, tolerating seasonal flooding. Minor damage from grasshoppers may occur. Over the winter it must go dormant to maintain strong growth but needs no special care where hardy. It is native to Europe, Asia, and northern Africa. Zones 4–8.

Cyperus prolifer
Dwarf papyrus
This compact plant has tight tufts of green strands atop its many stems. It looks like standard *Cyperus papyrus*, only about one-tenth the size, and is perfect for a tub garden or tabletop pond. Give it sun to part shade and moist soil or water to 4 inches (10 cm) deep. The plant reaches 12–18 inches (30–45 cm) tall and spreads 6–12 inches (15–30 cm). Overwinter it indoors in a sunny spot and keep soil moist at all times, but do not submerge the crown. Keep winter temperatures above 50°F (10°C). Native to eastern Africa and Madagascar, this species is sometimes confused with *C. haspan*, but true *C. haspan* is native to Florida and is not really ornamental, more weedy than not. Synonym *C. isocladus*. Earned Royal Horticultural Society Award of Garden Merit in 2002. Zones 9–11.

Decodon verticillatus
Swamp loosestrife, water willow
Leaves of this very showy plant are lance-shaped and grouped around each squarish stem in sets of twos or threes. Blooms are a purplish pink and sit close to the leaf axils, borne in summer along the stems as they arch over the water. Seeds form soon after. Stems become woody as they mature, rooting and forming new plants where they arch into the water, but the plant is not invasive. Fall color is blazing red-orange and yellow. The plant looks like a cross between *Buddleja* and purple loosestrife (*Lythrum salicaria*).

Excellent in large ponds and lakes, where it can be used as a hedge, much like burning bush (*Euonymus elatus*), *Decodon verticillatus* also makes a good single specimen. It grows 4 feet (1.2 m) tall and spreads 4–6 feet (1.2–1.8 m). Grow it in sun to part shade in wet soil or water to 2 feet (60 cm) deep. The species is native to North America, from Florida and Louisiana to Maine and Ontario, westward into Illinois. No special care or protection is needed for overwintering as the plant fares well in colder climates. Japanese beetles and various other beetles may be a problem, but none will kill it outright. Zones 3–9.

Dichromena colorata
White top sedge

The seed bracts resemble 3-inch (7.5-cm) white stars floating above grassy foliage. The flowers are very small and fuzzy, clustered at the center of the bract. After a time, both the flowers and the surrounding spikes turn light brown, retaining their starlike appearance. They make excellent cut arrangements and also dry well. Because they tolerate a wide range of moisture regimes, from fully submerged in spring floods to hot and dry in the summer, the plants are a great addition to detention ponds and wet grassy areas.

This tender aquatic species is native to North America, with a natural range that extends from Virginia into Florida and westward into Texas, where it grows in loose sods. It has a running habit and is best confined to a pot. It will reach a height of 12–24 inches (30–60 cm). Situate it in sun to part shade in moist soil or water to 1 inch (2.5 cm) deep. It requires no special care or maintenance and appreciates monthly doses of fertilizer. It overwinters well in a greenhouse or sunny room in the house. Synonym *Rhynchospora colorata*. Zones 8–11.

Decodon verticillatus

Dichromena colorata

Dulichium arundinaceum
Dwarf water bamboo,
three-way sedge

This plant is only 3 feet (90 cm) tall. True to one of its common names, it has upright, bright green foliage that resembles bamboo, with thin, tapered leaves that stand away from the stems at sharp angles. Another common name refers to the leaves' tendency to grow in three distinct directions around the stem, a habit apparent by looking straight down on the stem from above. Looking closer will reveal that the leaves spiral in a clockwise direction on some stems, but counterclockwise on others. It is not a true sedge since its stems are round and hollow, not triangular as the sedges are. The flowers are not showy. Instead, the plant produces small brown tassels along the top third of each stem in summer.

Dwarf water bamboo grows well in full sun or full shade, an added bonus for water gardeners searching for distinctive plants for a shaded pond. It reaches 12–14 inches (30–35 cm) tall in sun, taking on a yellow cast, but stays a deep green and reaches 36 inches (90 cm) tall in shade. It forms an excellent background to shorter, more showy plants, such as bacopas and alternantheras.

Native to North America, from Newfoundland and British Columbia south to Florida and California, dwarf water bamboo has a running habit but resents being transplanted. It can survive a solid freeze provided it is kept in the water. Grow it in moist soil or water to 2 inches (5 cm) deep. Zones 5–11.

'Tigress' has clean white margins on each leaf and white, not brown, seed heads. It is very attractive and highly ornamental.

ECHINODORUS
Melon sword

Many *Echinodorus* species are grown as aquarium plants because of their attractive underwater appearance. Water gardeners find them interesting for their out-of-water look. The white flowers bloom in summer, or year-round where active growth can take place. The plants are easy to grow and require little maintenance, though they quickly outgrow their pots and benefit from repotting every few years. Plants generally overwinter well in cool regions but in areas of considerable frost should be brought indoors to a greenhouse or warm sunny room for the winter. Mealybugs can be a problem in winter.

Echinodorus species are native to many of the warmer regions of the Americas. When not in flower, they can be difficult to distinguish from water plantain (*Alisma*). To tell them apart, gently squeeze the leaf stem. Melon sword has stiff, triangular stems, while water plantain has soft, more rounded stems.

Dulichium arundinaceum 'Tigress'

Echinodorus cordifolius

This elegant aquatic has all the characteristics for which melon sword is known—clusters of large spoon-shaped leaves and sprays of white summertime flowers that resemble cascades of single roses. The plant grows in a clump and keeps to itself, not trying to force its presence upon other parts of the pond. Native to the central and southern United States and into Mexico, this species grows naturally as a submerged or marginal plant in the southern regions of the Mississippi River. It takes sun to part shade and moist soil or water to 6 inches (15 cm) deep, growing 24–36 inches (60–90 cm) tall and spreading 36 inches (90 cm). Synonym *Echinodorus radicans*. Zones 5b–11.

'**Marble Queen**' has showy creamy white patches on its leaves, adding more beauty to an already noteworthy plant. Just as floriferous as the all-green species, it has white flowers about 1 inch (2.5 cm) across. This selection can grow submerged and will tolerate seasonal flooding. It reaches 12–24 inches (30–60 cm) tall and spreads 24 inches (60 cm). Zones 5b–11.

Echinodorus palaefolius
Giant melon sword

This giant has the largest leaves of the melon swords, about 18 inches (45 cm) across. Round and cup-shaped, the leaves rise to 3 feet (90 cm). The flower stalks reach 5 feet (1.5 m) tall and

Echinodorus palaefolius

Echinodorus cordifolius

Echinodorus cordifolius 'Marble Queen'

bear hundreds of 2-inch (5-cm) flowers all summer long. Zone 9.

ELEOCHARIS
Hair grass

The genus *Eleocharis* comprises 150 species, including varieties that can be found virtually everywhere in the world. Many of these species are aquatic, growing emerged in the shallow waters of marshes, ponds, and streams. They grow from rhizomes or stolons and bear brown spikelets that look something like heads on a matchstick. Many species are native to North America. They are distinguished by the shape of their leaves and, most especially, by the size and shape of their mature fruit (spikelets and nutlets). Several species have long been used as food crops for their rhizomes that are high in carbohydrates,

Eleocharis dulcis

Eleocharis acicularis

Epilobium hirsutum

such as water chestnut (*E. dulcis*). Large stands of *Eleocharis* help to prevent soil erosion and provide cover to amphibians at the shoreline.

Eleocharis species most commonly available to water gardeners are emergent forms with the characteristic straight stems topped with brown heads. Submerged selections are also cultivated for aquariums and may be grown as oxygenating plants in the pond. In the water landscape, *Eleocharis* makes an unusual accent plant. It provides an upright, architectural backdrop for shorter, creeping plants. It is easy to grow and requires little care. Cold-tolerant species will usually withstand being frozen in the pond and need not be put to the lowest depths of the water garden. More tender selections should be submerged to avoid freezing temperatures. Voles and mice love to overwinter in thick blankets of these plants.

Eleocharis acicularis
Needle rush hair grass
Thin blades of grasslike foliage resemble red fescue (*Festuca rubra*), the main component of seed sold for shady lawns. Summertime flowers are green. This species is great along the shore or in detention ponds needing a grasslike plant to hold the soil, yet one that is mowable and can take light traffic. This species forms excellent sod. Grow it in sun to part shade in moist soil, or grow it submerged. It reaches 12 inches (30 cm) high and has a running spread that will cover about 12 inches (30 cm) square in a season in the Chicago area. Geese are really hard on this plant, feeding on it in spring. The species is native to North America. Zones 3–11.

Eleocharis dulcis
Chinese water chestnut
Native to tropical Asia, this is the plant that yields the water chestnuts used in stir-fries. It grows like green drinking straws, forming bright green tufts 24–36 inches (60–90 cm) tall. Each tuft will spread no more than 12 inches (30 cm), but each plant will produce many tufts depending on heat and fertilizer. Brown flowers appear in summer.

Situate the plant in sun to part shade in moist soil or water to 6 inches (15 cm) deep. Overwinter it indoors as a houseplant or dry down the tubers that form on the ends of the rhizomes and store them in a moist but not wet place. Synonym *Eleocharis tuberosa*. Zones 8–11.

Epilobium hirsutum
Pink water jewel
Native to Europe, this moisture-loving perennial needs moist to wet soil and is tolerant of seasonal flooding. Situate it in sun to part shade. It grows 18 inches (45 cm) tall and spreads 6 inches (15 cm). With pink flowers blooming in summer, it is a great performer in wet gardens and marginal plantings. White and pale pink forms are also available. Zones 5–7.

EQUISETUM
Horsetail, scouring rush
Of the roughly 30 species of *Equisetum*, only a few are truly aquatic, although several will adapt well to wet soils. They grow wild in most temperate areas of the world and are easily identified by their straight, hollow stems, which are grooved. Each joint is a distinct part of the stem and has a black band at its edge. Most species will survive freezing temperatures and last through the winter at the edge of the pond, leaving no need to move them below the frost line. Equisetums are grazed by wildfowl, muskrats, and moose, and they are an important food source for breeding trumpeter swans.

Equisetum fluviatile
Water horsetail
A true aquatic, *Equisetum fluviatile* requires water to survive—from fully moist soil to floating—and will not invade its terrestrial neighbors. It has green stalks with large black bands accented by thin pink bands. This species will sprout from stem sections that contain a joint when the section is floated in water. Native to Canada and the Great Lakes area, south to Indiana, water horsetail branches freely and grows very thin, long side shoots that radiate from each

Equisetum fluviatile

Eriophorum vaginatum

Equisetum hyemale

Glyceria maxima 'Variegata'

main stem. Stems are not perennial like those of *E. hyemale*. Grow water horsetail in sun to shade. It reaches 24 inches (60 cm) tall with a running spread. Coots may feed on it in the spring. Zones 4–11.

Equisetum hyemale
Common horsetail

This species of *Equisetum* grows equally well in wet or dry soil, but not with its crown under the waterline. It can be a bit of a thug in the garden because of its running habit, and so is best always kept in a pot. Stems often remain green throughout the winter, even in colder climates. Grow it in sun to part shade. It reaches 24 inches (60 cm) tall and has a running spread. The species is native from Newfoundland to Guatemala. Zones 4–11.

'Robustum' is larger than the species by a third with thicker stems up to 1/2 inch (12 mm) across.

Eriophorum vaginatum
Hare's tail cotton grass

Despite its common name, this species is a sedge, not a grass, with sharply edged triangular leaves. Hairlike white tufts of perianth bristles on the flower heads continue all summer, and the thin, grasslike foliage grows in dense clumps. The species does best in cooler climates and is not a stout water plant in regions with hot, muggy summers. Circumboreal in the Northern Hemisphere, it is native to bogs, growing best in neutral to acidic water. It will not tolerate ponds with alkaline water. It often grows wild in cranberry bogs with other acid-loving plants and shrubs, and is very useful in large groups, like in a wet meadow or carnivorous plant bog. It is best grown in a container, if not designed to be a drift, or it will look rather sparse.

Gray-green foliage stops just below the flower heads, setting off their orange or rust color. This species sends out runners to start new tussocks, creating the look of a tussock that is more broad and dense than the open sod of other species. The seed heads are dense, having one, not multiple, tufts. Grow plants in full sun in wet soil or under 2 inches (5 cm) of water. They can take seasonal flooding in spring when, because the water is colder, it holds more oxygen. Plants grow 12–20 inches (30–50 cm) tall with a spread of 12 inches (30 cm). Hare's tail cotton grass usually overwinters well at the edge of the pond. Although voles and mice love most cotton grasses and will eat any parts that are not submerged, this species does not seem to be bothered by these pests. Zones (3)4–5.

Glyceria maxima 'Variegata'
Variegated manna grass

The leaves of this rambling aquatic are narrow, only 2 inches (5 cm) wide, usually 12 inches (30 cm) or so in height, and striped in creamy white and bright green. In the spring and fall, when the weather is cool, the leaves take on a delightful pink tinge. Flowers are negligible tan blooms in summer. A strong grower in the moist to wet soil or water to 1 inch (2.5 cm) deep that it prefers, variegated manna grass runs freely and should be restrained in a pot so that it does not interfere with its neighbors. In larger earthen plantings, it should be kept in check by pulling. Grow it in sun to part shade. This cold-tolerant manna grass overwinters easily in the pond. It requires winter submersion beneath only enough water to cover the crown of the plant, with no need to move it deeper into the pond. Reversion to its all-green form is not uncommon but is easily corrected by removing the rhizomes from which the green leaves have sprouted. Mice and voles are usually a problem in winter, and coots in spring. Synonym *Glyceria aquatica* 'Variegata'. Zones 4–11.

HIBISCUS
Mallow

Large summertime flowers lasting but a day are borne on shrubby plants up to 6 feet (1.8 m) high, depending on the species. The flowers are generally red to white, usually with a strong eye zone of color. The tropical forms are more vibrant in color than the other species. After flowering, hibiscus develop papery-covered green fruits that some people find attractive. The plants die to the ground in winter, growing again in the spring and summer. Many new varieties are released every year; give them a try.

Hibiscus militaris
Halberd-leafed marsh mallow

This large shrubby plant has an open vase shape. The slightly rounded, large, 4- to 6-inch (10- to 15-cm) flowers are more tubular than flat and pink to white, generally with a rose eye. The leaves are distinct in that they have two short lobes on either side of a much longer center lobe. This species is native throughout the eastern United States from Illinois to Florida to Texas. Grow it in full sun for best flowering, growth, and shape; the plant tends to get floppy in shady sites. It reaches 4–6 feet (1.2–1.8 m) tall and spreads 4 feet (1.2 m). Grow it in moist soil or water to 2 feet (60 cm) deep. It also tolerates

seasonal flooding and is great for detention basins. Weevils and aphids can be problems for this species. Zone 5 and up.

Hibiscus moscheutos
Water hibiscus, swamp mallow

This medium-sized shrub has stunning 10- to 12-inch (25- to 30-cm) flowers ranging from white through deep red, with or without eye zones. It prefers moist soil or water to 4 inches (10 cm) deep, though it will tolerate seasonal flooding and even dry soil. It also tolerates brackish water up to 15 parts per million and is very adaptable from alkaline to acidic conditions. It grows well in sun to part shade, but is best in full sun. Height ranges from 24 inches (60 cm) for the dwarf selections to more than 6 feet (180 cm) for standard plants. Spread is 2–4 feet (60–120 cm). Highly variable over its North American range,

Hibiscus militaris

Hibiscus moscheutos 'Kopper King'

Hibiscus moscheutos

Hibiscus moscheutos 'Lord Baltimore'

this species is found in the northeastern United States through to Illinois and south to Florida.

Water hibiscus is very easy to grow and performs well in a planting, needing little care. It is excellent along lakeshores and streams, in seasonally flooded areas, in detention areas, and along retention ponds. Cut back the stems for the winter and mulch plants heavily where they are not hardy. Plants may be slow to reappear in the spring. They attracts butterflies and even hummingbirds, and do not seem to be bothered by weevils or aphids. Zone 5 and up.

'Anne Arundel', strong, true pink.

'Blue River', clear white.

'Fantasia', soft pink.

'Fire Ball', red with red foliage.

'Flare', fuchsia red and sterile.

'Kopper King', red foliage and white flowers with rose radiating from a carmine eye.

'Lady Baltimore', pink with a wide carmine eye.

'Lord Baltimore', red. Probably a selection or hybrid of *Hibiscus coccineus*, though usually sold as a selection of *H. moscheutos*.

'Moy Grande', 12-inch (30-cm) rose-pink flowers.

'Old Yella', cream.

'Sweet Caroline', ruffled pink.

'Turn of the Century', pinwheel of rose and white.

Hottonia palustris

Native to Europe and Asia, this delightful plant roots at the edge of the pond and then floats out onto the water surface. Leaves of this unusual marginal are thin and deeply cut, arising as a whorl from a central rosette. Flowers look like tiny primula blossoms, usually white or lilac with a yellow throat, and bloom in summer. The plant grows in sun to shade in water 12–24 inches (30–60 cm) deep. It is best in softer water. It reaches a height of 4 inches (10 cm) above the water surface and spreads 4–12 inches (10–30 cm). Overwintering takes no special care where the plant is hardy; where it must be brought in, keep it potted in a cool place, like a refrigerator. China mark moth and aphids can be problems. Zone 6 and up.

Hottonia palustris

Hydrocotyle sibthorpioides 'Variegata'

Hydrocotyle sibthorpioides 'Variegata'
Crystal confetti

This dainty plant forms a full carpet of frilled, heart-shaped, jade green leaves that are edged in cream. As the plant matures, the foliage develops pink margins and burgundy stems. Because it is just 1 inch (2.5 cm) tall and trails freely, it is excellent for container water gardens, where the soil can stay evenly moist to wet. Crystal confetti is also perfect for waterfalls or in bogs or in aquatic topiary. It is more shade tolerant than other pennyworts, taking sun to full shade. The species is native to Japan and China. Treat it as a houseplant where it is not hardy. Zones 6 (with cover) to 10.

HYGROPHILA
Hygro, temple plant

Hygrophila is a confusing genus of several species all sold interchangeably as the same plant. Many are sold as aquarium plants, some of which are also suitable as marginal plants in the water garden. Native to Southeast Asia, the species have leaves that are usually long and thin, wider toward the middle, and opposite. Plants grow in sun to shade.

Hygrophila corymbosa 'Stricta'
Dragon lanterns

An upright, fast-growing plant with foliage tinted in purple when the weather is cool, in spring and fall, this very free-flowering cultivar is often covered with clusters of tiny blue flowers looking like turtles' heads sitting near the central stem. The plant reaches 12 inches (30 cm) high and wide, though in shade it will grow to 36 inches (90 cm) tall. Grow it in moist soil or submerged. Where it is not hardy, bring it indoors and treat it as a houseplant for the winter, keeping it wet. Spider mites may attack in the winter, but simply submerge the plant for a few days to kill them. Zones 9–11.

Hygrophila difformis
Water wisteria

Water wisteria has mintlike foliage and tiny blue flowers borne at the leaf joints on long, trailing

Hygrophila corymbosa 'Stricta'

stems. When the leaves are grown submerged, they become ferny and very finely cut. When grown above the water, the foliage is very sticky. Water wisteria is great in containers and in the margins of ornamental ponds to hide pots. Grow it in sun to just part shade in moist soil or water to 2 inches (5 cm) deep. It reaches 6–10 inches (15–25 cm) tall and has a running spread. Aphids may appear in late summer. Overwinter it inside as a houseplant or in an aquarium. Zones 9–11.

'Variegata' (variegated water wisteria) has white striping in submerged leaves and slight mottling in emerged leaves.

Hygrophila difformis

Hymenocallis liriosome
Spider lily

Showy, fragrant flowers are up to 7 inches (18 cm) wide, having a long tube and then six lobes and a cup, or crown, of white from which stamens rise. They look like spiders because of their long petals and sepals. Leaves are narrow, less than 1 inch (2.5 cm) wide, and 12 inches (30 cm) or more in length. Like *Amaryllis*, *Hymenocallis* has long, straplike, deeply grooved leaves. The plant reaches a height of 18 inches (45 cm) and spreads to 24 inches (60 cm), making nice clumps. Grow it in sun to part shade in moist soil or water to 2 inches (5 cm) over the crown. It tolerates seasonal flooding very well. To overwinter spider lily in colder climates, dig up bulbs and store in a cool, dry place. Some people recommend leaving the soil on the bulbs and storing them dry in a bag or box in a cool dry place not above 60°F (16°C). Or, bring them indoors in a pot and treat as a houseplant. The species is native to Louisiana and Texas. Zones 7–11.

Hymenocallis liriosome

Ipomoea aquatica
Water spinach, water morning glory

The young shoots are often used in stir-fries. The 3-inch (7.5-cm) white flowers appear in late spring or early summer and again in early fall when the weather cools and days become shorter. This native of tropical Asia is considered a noxious weed in warmer climates for its ability to grow very rapidly on the water surface. Do not plant it in sites that are connected to

Ipomoea aquatica

natural bodies of water; it must not be allowed to spread. It grows fast to help shade a pond and can tolerate koi predation.

The plant grows 8–10 inches (20–25 cm) high in sun to part shade and has a running, floating spread. When rooted to the bottom, it grows in water 4–18 inches (10–45 cm) deep; in deeper water it forms floating mats. In colder climates, bring in new shoots and grow them in a bowl of warm water in a sunny room. Or plant the new shoots in hanging baskets by a sunny window. Water spinach almost stops growing in winter when the days are short, then resumes when the days get longer in spring. Mealybugs and spider mites may attack in winter, but simply submerge the plant for a few days to control. Zones 9–11.

JUNCUS
Rush
The stiff, hollow, strongly upright foliage of many *Juncus* species provides a useful background for other pondside plants with a bolder or more delicate nature. Flowers appear as brown tassels that droop from near or at the tip of the leaves. Most *Juncus* species have little or few leaves and are noted for their long, spiked stems. These are usually dark green, but light blue selections are also available. Foliage dries well and the plants are much favored in floral arrangements. In many climates the foliage will be evergreen throughout the winter. Stands of *Juncus* are useful in earthen ponds as spawning ground for bluegills and sunnies. Dragonfly larvae often cling to the foliage while they metamorphose into adult dragonflies. Rushes provide important shelter to fish, fowl, and insects.

Cold-tolerant *Juncus* species may be overwintered in the pond with no need to be placed at the bottom with waterlilies or lotus. Tender species may be brought indoors and kept as houseplants.

Juncus effusus
Common rush, soft rush
A good vertical accent plant, the circumboreal common rush has stiff spines of green foliage that often retain their color all year long, even in colder climates. Grow it in sun to part shade in moist soil or water to 4 inches (10 cm) deep. It does best if the water level drops in the summer to just wet soil. Plants reach 24–36 inches (60–90 cm) tall and 12 inches (30 cm) wide. Zones 3–11.

'**Gold Strike**' has gold striping along the length of its dark green foliage.

'**Lemon Twist**' is a twisted version of 'Gold Strike'. A bright gold stripe covering about a quarter of the diameter of the blade runs up every curl.

'**Spiralis**' (true corkscrew rush) has tightly coiled foliage that is excellent in fresh or dry floral arrangements. It grows to 12–18 inches (30–45 cm) high and wide and is almost evergreen even in colder climates. This cultivar is good as an accent for bolder foliage like that of *Pontederia*.

Juncus effusus

'Unicorn' (giant corkscrew rush) has dark green, twisted foliage that is much larger and taller, at 24 inches (60 cm) high and wide, than that of true corkscrew rush. It retains its bold shape and texture throughout the summer and even into the fall and winter.

Juncus ensifolius
Flat sedge, dagger leaf

The broad leaves look like small *Iris* seedlings. With slightly blue-green leaves and dark black-brown seed heads all summer, this species is great when used with irises and other finer-foliaged plants. Grow it in sun to shade in moist soil or water to 2 inches (5 cm) deep. It tolerates seasonal flooding. Plants reach 10–20 inches (25–50 cm) tall and 12 inches (30 cm). wide. The species is found mostly across Canada and the upper U.S. Midwest, to Alaska and south to California. Grasshoppers may attack it. Zone 4 and up.

Juncus filiformis
Thread rush

Often sold as *Juncus effusus* 'Spiralis' in the nursery trade, thread rush is a nice alternative to that coarser plant. It is native to the northern United States. Grow it in sun to shade and moist soil or water to 4 inches (10 cm) deep. Plant height is 12–18 inches (30–60 cm), with a spread of 12 inches (30 cm). The plant needs to go dormant to stay healthy. Zone 3 and up.

'Blonde Ambition' is an almost completely yellow selection, with about a quarter of the blade still green. It has semilax leaves and really brightens up an area. Usually listed as a selection of *Juncus effusus*, it is a real treat for the pond.

Juncus ensifolius

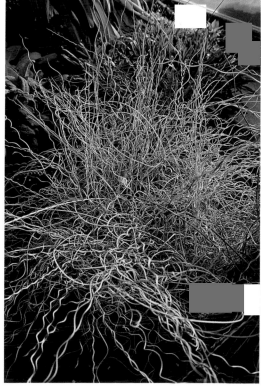

Juncus filiformis 'Blonde Ambition'

Juncus glaucus

Juncus inflexus 'Afro'

Juncus glaucus
Blue rush
The upright, baby blue leaves resemble fescue (*Festuca*) at the edge of the pond and persist all winter for great off-season interest. Grow it in full sun in moist soil or water to 2 inches (5 cm) deep. The plant reaches 12–24 inches (30–60 cm) high and 24 inches (60 cm) wide. The species is native to Europe. Zones 4–11. .

Juncus inflexus
Hard rush, European hard rush
Juncus inflexus appears more narrowly upright and gray-green (though some forms are quite blue) than the common rush, *J. effusus*. The tubular foliage resembles that of *J. glaucus* but is larger and more dramatic. Grow it in sun to part shade in moist soil or water to 4 inches (10 cm) deep. Plant height is 24–36 inches (30–90 cm), plant width is 18 inches (45 cm). In the fall, cold weather causes some of the green forms to turn dark purple. The species is native to Europe and other temperate regions of the world. Zones 5–11.

'Afro' (blue medusa corkscrew rush) has billowy curls of powdery blue foliage that make the perfect accent for ponds, streams, waterfalls, and even the moist perennial or bog garden. Ever blue even in colder climates, blue medusa is a marked improvement over standard corkscrew rush, *Juncus effusus* 'Spiralis'. The foliage has better substance, holding its curled form longer. The plant grows 12–18 inches (30–45 cm) tall and spreads 24 inches (60 cm).

'Lovesick Blues' (weeping blue hard rush) produces gray-blue pendant foliage.

Juncus patens
California gray rush
This tender, clump-forming rush has stiff, dark gray, slender foliage just 1/8 to 3/16 inch (4–5 mm) in diameter. It is excellent in pots. Although it grows in sun to shade, it has a tendency to flop in too much shade. It prefers moist soil or water to 6 inches (15 cm) deep. Plant height is 18–30 inches (45–75 cm), plant width is 24 inches (60 cm). The species is native to California

and, some experts say, along the Pacific Rim, including Japan, China, Korea, Russia, and Alaska. Zones 6–11.

'**Carman's Gray**' is a fantastic, widely popular rush. Plants are often grown from seed, so some are not as nice as the original.

'**Elk Blue**' is a worthy cultivar discovered by Randy Baldwin in the hills southeast of Elk, California.

'**Quartz Creek**', a selection from southern Oregon, reaches a height of 24–36 inches (60–90 cm) and spreads slowly to 24–36 inches (60–90 cm) wide.

Juncus patens

Justicia americana
Water willow

Much underused in the water garden and in wetland reclamation projects, *Justicia americana* is very attractive, easy to care for, and free-flowering. It is an excellent plant to control soil erosion and is great in streams and other areas that have wave action or moving water. *Justicia americana* produces masses of 1-inch (2.5-cm) clusters of white to pink-purple flowers in summer. Foliage is narrow, like willow leaves, and grows on shrubby plants 12–18 inches (30–45 cm) high and 12 inches (30 cm) wide. Grow it in full sun or part shade in moist soil or in water up to 10 inches (25 cm) deep, so creating a "fishable edge" in the earth-bottom pond. Overwinter it in the pond, it does not need to be submerged. The species is native to eastern North America, from Ontario and Quebec south to Georgia and Texas, and westward to Oklahoma and Wisconsin. Zones 4–11.

Justicia americana

Lilium michiganense
Michigan lily

This midwestern native has large, recurved, red-orange petals on tall plants that resemble small-flowered tiger lilies. Plants grow 24–60 inches (60–150 cm) high and produce as few as one or as many as 25 flowers each. The flowers are 4–5 inches (10–13 cm) across, generally orange with red throats and red spots. Grow it in sun to shade in wet to evenly moist soil. It tolerates seasonal inundation. Michigan lily is great along a shady

Lilium michiganense in the wild

Lobelia cardinalis

stream. Selections have been made in different colors, but it takes some searching to find them. Yellows, reds, and spot-free forms exist.

LOBELIA

A favorite of the bog and perennial garden, lobelias are cherished for their brilliant flowers, which appear in late summer through fall. Flower petals are divided in half, with two tips pointing upward and three pointing downward, somewhat like a split-petaled snapdragon. Leaves are narrow and grow alternately on a central stem. The plant does not usually branch, each stem growing from a separate crown. *Lobelia* species range from less than 1 foot to 5 feet (30–150 cm) tall. They attract butterflies and hummingbirds, which help in pollination. Some species are not reliably hardy in cold climates. It is best to place them deep in the pond for the winter or to mulch them well in the perennial bed. Sometimes they will not return in the spring despite a gardener's best efforts.

Lobelia cardinalis
Cardinal flower
This species is known for its bright crimson flowers on single stems that reach up to 3 feet (90 cm) high. Spread is 1 foot (30 cm). Leaves are ovate, clothing the stems until the terminal flower spikes occur. Grow it in sun to part shade in moist soil or water to 3 inches (7.5 cm) deep. The species is native to North America and often hybridized with *Lobelia siphilitica* to produce plants with spectacular flower color. Earned Royal Horticultural Society Award of Garden Merit in 1993. Zones 5–11, but Zone 3 with snow cover.

Lobelia siphilitica
Giant blue lobelia
Native to fens of eastern North America, giant blue lobelia is very similar to cardinal flower in form and habit. Leaves are slightly more lance-shaped and irregularly toothed. Flowers are bright blue. Flower spikes are densely covered with blooms. Grow it in sun to part shade in

Lobelia siphilitica

moist soil or water to 3 inches (7.5 cm) deep. It performs best in neutral or alkaline soil. Plants reach 12–36 inches (30–90 cm) high and spread 12 inches (30 cm). Zones 3–11.

'**Alba**' (giant white lobelia) is a popular white-flowered selection.

'**Nana**' is a dwarf selection.

LUDWIGIA
Water primrose
Ludwigia species range in size from more than 8 feet (2.5 m) tall to less than 6 inches (15 cm) tall. They are almost cosmopolitan, occurring in most parts of the world. Leaves are usually rounded,

Ludwigia arcuta

Ludwigia arcuta 'Grandiflora'

Ludwigia peploides

toothed, and shiny. Flowers are mostly yellow, single, flat, and four-petaled. Plants grow in sun to part shade in moist soil or water to varying depths. Frost-tender species are best overwintered as houseplants in colder climates.

Ludwigia arcuta
Primrose creeper

A great pond cover, primrose creeper creates an unusual visual effect in the water garden. As it floats out over the water, it holds the last 6 inches (15 cm) or so of its foliage straight up from the water surface. Summertime flowers are a cheerful, bright yellow, about 1 inch (2.5 cm) wide. Grow it in water to 2 inches (5 cm) deep. Plant spread is 12–24 inches (30–60 cm). Zones 6–11.

'Grandiflora' has many more flowers than the standard form of the species.

Ludwigia peploides
Dwarf primrose creeper

A creeping form, this species has yellow-orange flowers of 1–1-1/2 inches (2.5–4 cm). Grow it in moist soil or water to 3 inches (7.5 cm) deep. The plant reaches 4–6 inches (10–15 cm) tall and spreads 2–4 feet (60–120 cm). Zones 8–11.

Ludwigia peruviana
Sunshine bush

This shrubby form can grow into a small tree 2–8 feet (60–250 cm) high in a single season. It has 1- to 2-inch (2.5- to 5-cm) flowers all summer long. Grow it in full sun to part shade in water to 10 inches (25 cm) deep. It spreads 2–8 feet (60–250 cm). Sunshine bush is great in containers or large ponds. Zones 9–11.

Lychnis flos-cuculi
Ragged robin

Leaves of this wet-tolerant perennial are narrow, just 1/2 inch (12 mm) wide, and 2–3 inches (5–7.5 cm) long. Flowers rise above the base of the plant on tall, 12- to 24-inch (30- to 60-cm), arching stems. White or pink finely cut blooms of 1/2–3/4 inch (12–18 mm) appear at the tip in a cluster. This very delicate plant is

Ludwigia peruviana

Lychnis flos-cuculi

Lysichiton americanum

delightful in moist soil at the edge of the pond margin or in the bog garden. It tolerates about a week of high water, as in drainage basins. In sun it grows to 10 inches (25 cm) tall, in part shade to 24 inches (60 cm). Plant spread is 10 inches (25 cm). Because ragged robin is not particularly cold tolerant, it should be heavily mulched. The foliage is evergreen and is damaged below 10°F (-12°C). This European native has naturalized in eastern North America. Zones 5–8.

'Jenny' has pink flowers.

'Nana' is a dwarf form available in both white and pink. It grows to only 4–6 inches (10–15 cm) tall and wide.

Lysichiton americanum
Yellow skunk cabbage

Lysichitons are noted for their large, rippled leaves and unusual "hoods" that cloak spathes of flowers in early spring, often as the leaves are only just starting to break through the soil. As the flowers pass away, the foliage takes center stage. The common name comes from the musky odor released when the leaves or flowers are crushed. The sap from the leaves and roots can make your hands itch. Plants are very striking in damp shade, often growing among trees along streambeds and creeks. They overwinter well in northern climates and need no special care or protection.

The "hood" of *Lysichiton americanum* is bright yellow. The plant grows to 10 inches (25 cm) high and about 3–5 inches (7.5–13 cm) wide. Leaves appear later and reach 3–4 feet (90–120 cm) tall. Grow it in part shade in moist soil. Plant spread is 3–4 feet (90–120 cm). Striking at the edge of a stream or pond, this native of western North America, from Alaska southward into California and eastward to Montana, tolerates seasonal flooding. It is best planted under a canopy of deciduous trees to provide shade during the heat of summer. Zones 4–7. Earned Royal Horticultural Society Award of Garden Merit in 1993.

LYSIMACHIA

Lysimachia is a cheerful clan of moisture-loving plants that usually have yellow flowers in summer. Blooms are located at or near the leaf axils, but flower shape varies considerably among the different species. Many adapt well to the perennial border, although they grow equally well in sun to part shade at the margins of the pond or in container water gardens. *Lysimachia* species are native to temperate regions of the Northern Hemisphere. Most species are cold tolerant and require no special protection through the winter.

Lysimachia nummularia
Creeping Jenny

An excellent ground cover for the edge of the water garden or pond, creeping Jenny also is well suited to scramble down a waterfall or tumble from the edge of a tub garden. It grows to 1 inch (2.5 cm) high and creeps in moist soil or water to 1 inch deep (2.5 cm). The rounded leaves clasp on opposite sides of its stem, forming a tight, dense chain of foliage. Yellow flowers appear in the summer, with rounded petals that form open blooms held at the leaf axils. Native to Europe, this species is widely naturalized in many parts of the world. Zones 4–10.

'Aurea' (golden creeping Jenny), a variegated form, is very popular for its clear yellow foliage. It does not flower as freely as the species. Earned Royal Horticultural Society Award of Garden Merit in 1993.

Lysimachia terrestris
Swamp candles

A tall, showy species, this North American native grows as far south as Georgia. Plant height is 8–18 inches (20–45 cm) and spread is 6 inches (15 cm). Flowers are borne terminally, comprising the top 4–6 inches (10–15 cm) of the plant. Some forms have a red eye in the flowers. In full sun, the plant is shorter; in full shade, taller. Grow it in moist soil or water to 2–6 inches (5–15 cm) deep. Lightly branching, it forms loose stands somewhat like lizard tail (*Saururus cernuus*). It has bright yellow fall color. Zones 4–9.

Lysimachia nummularia

Lysimachia terrestris

Lysimachia thyrsiflora
Tufts of gold

Smaller than other upright species, this wetland plant has thin, 1/2-inch (12-mm) wide leaves that are ovate and pointed, about 2 inches (5 cm) long. Flowers look like tufts of yellow, held near the stem and leaf axil. They appear in midspring and last for several days. In the fall, withered stems turn a brilliant yellow. The species is excellent for the front of the bog garden or at the edge of the stream and makes a good companion to *Asclepias incarnata* and *Iris virginica* in detention areas. Grow it in moist soil or water to 6 inches (15 cm) deep. It reaches 12 inches (30 cm) high and wide. Zones 5–8.

Marsilea mutica

A delightful addition to the water garden, *Marsilea mutica* is one of several water clovers considered the lucky charms of the pond. The clover-shaped foliage belies the fact that it is really a fern. Like all the water clovers, *M. mutica* is grown for its attractive four-lobed foliage and ease of care, not for any floral attributes, but only *M. mutica* has leaves that float on the water. The emerged leaves open in the morning and close at night, giving the appearance of many small butterflies at rest. In very cold climates, overwinter by bringing it indoors and keeping it as a houseplant. Zones 5–11.

'Micro Mini' has leaves about the size of a dime that float on the water surface or rise slightly above it. The plant is ideal for container water gardens. Dense growth can reach 3 inches (7.5 cm) high, but usually is no more than 1 inch (2.5 cm) above the soil line. The plant has a running spread. Grow it in sun to shade in moist soil or water to 4 inches (10 cm) deep. Probably three different plants are sold under this name.

Lysimachia thyrsiflora

Marsilea mutica

Marsilea mutica 'Micro Mini'

Mentha aquatica
Aquatic mint

Mentha species are highly fragrant and have long been used for their aromatic qualities. Native to Europe, these garden mints have been introduced into many parts of the world, including North America. Many other mints are native across the Northern Hemisphere.

Mentha aquatica, always a favorite with water gardeners, requires wet conditions to grow and prosper. The attractive, even-green leaves are lance-shaped, lobed, toothed, and often hairy, especially on the bottom. They can be used in teas and jams. The flowers are clustered balls of lavender-pink surrounding the stemlike little pom-poms. Blossoms appear in midsummer and continue until fall. They attract plenty of butterflies. When cool weather arrives, foliage turns purple. Because of its running habit, mint should be kept containerized for best effect. It will tolerate freezing temperatures and conditions, so no special care is required in colder climates. Grow it in sun to part shade in moist soil or water to 2 inches (5 cm) deep. It reaches 3–12 inches (7.5–30 cm) high with a running habit. Zones 5–11.

Mentha aquatica

Mimulus cardinalis
Red monkey flower

This great North American native has large, 1- to 2-inch (2.5- to 5-cm) flowers of tomato red to cherry red. Leaves are hairy and sticky, with prominent joints that look like knuckles. The plant grows in part shade and thrives in mountain sites that are sunny but cool in summer. It grows 24 inches (60 cm) tall and 12 inches (30 cm) wide in just wet soil. Aphids can sometimes be a problem, as well as a root rot fungus like fusarium when plants stressed. When conditions are right it is easy to grow. It does poorly in humid weather. In Yosemite National Park plants grow in dripping seeps on the mountainside. A yellow form is available. Zones 5–8, possibly 9 with shade.

Mimulus guttatus
Yellow monkey flower

Highly variable, this species may grow 6–36 inches (15–90 cm) high with a spread of 8–10 inches (20–25 cm). It is native throughout North America but not as cold tolerant as other species. The yellow flowers have the characteristic shape but are up to 1-1/2 inches (4 cm) in diameter. Grow the plant in part to full shade in moist soil or water to 1 inch (2.5 cm) deep. Zones 6–9.

'**Variegatus**' has gold splashes on its foliage and is very striking even when not in bloom. Synonym *Mimulus guttatus* 'Richard Bish'.

Mimulus 'Lothian Fire'
Red monkey flower

Although this plant may not be very tall, its bold flowers make a lasting impression. The blooms are bright red trumpets with yellow throats. They are well accented by shiny green leaves with red stems. The plant is stunning when cascading down a stream or waterfall. Give it sun to part shade and moist soil or water to 1 inch (2.5 cm) deep. It does best in moving water. Plant height and spread are 12 inches (30 cm). Zones 7–9.

Mimulus cardinalis

Mimulus 'Lothian Fire'

Mimulus guttatus

Mimulus ringens
Lavender monkey flower

This species grows freely through much of North America, from Nova Scotia to Georgia and into Texas. It has stalkless leaves that are oblong and somewhat toothed. Flowers are a lovely lavender color, varying from almost grape to almost white, peeking out from between the shiny jade green leaves. The plant blooms profusely and is great with *Asclepias*, *Juncus*, *Scirpus*, or sedges. Grow it in sun to part shade in water up to 6 inches (15 cm) deep. The plant reaches 20–30 inches (50–75 cm) high and 12–20 inches (30–50 cm) wide. Zones 5–11.

Mimulus ringens

Myosotis scorpioides
Water forget-me-not

This wetland species is a delightful front-of-the-pond margin plant that brings in the early summer with sprays of flowers resembling small, delicate, single roses. Color ranges from white to pink to light blue and bright blue, depending upon the cultivar. Plants grow to about 6 inches (15 cm) or so in height, spreading to about 12 inches (30 cm), with small, oblong leaves that are usually clear green and somewhat hairy. They form a dense mat that grows well not only at the edge of the water garden but also in a stream or by a waterfall.

After its first flowering, water forget-me-not will often flower intermittently throughout the summer as long as the weather stays cool. In warm, humid climates, the plants will wither some and leaves may turn dark, black, and crispy. Trim such leaves and wait until cooler days return. The plants will resprout and begin to rebloom. Native to Europe and Siberia. *Myosotis* species are widely naturalized in temperate regions, including North America. In the southern United States, they are best grown as winter annuals, much like pansies. In colder climates, however, they overwinter well.

Myosotis grows well in moving water, benefiting from the additional oxygen that comes with the flow of water through its roots. It is good for filtration and helps reduce the occurrence of green algae in the pond. Situate it in sun to part shade in moist soil or water to 1 inch (2.5 cm) deep. Zones 4–9.

'Mermaid' (blue water forget-me-not) has a more compact habit, slightly larger leaves, and larger blue flowers dotted with white eyes. It also is slightly more tender. Zones 5–9.

'Pinkie' (pink water forget-me-not) forms a creeping cushion of cotton-candy pink flowers with white eyes in spring. It is excellent for underplanting around larger marginals in the pond, or tucked into a pocket along a stream or waterfall. It also performs well in a table-top pond. Plant spread is smaller than the species at 6–10 inches (15–25 cm).

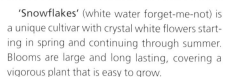

'Snowflakes' (white water forget-me-not) is a unique cultivar with crystal white flowers starting in spring and continuing through summer. Blooms are large and long lasting, covering a vigorous plant that is easy to grow.

'Wisconsin' (blue water forget-me-not) has blue flowers that fade to pink. It continues to flower off and on throughout the summer, and blooms heavier again in the fall. Zones 4–9.

Oenanthe javanica 'Flamingo'
Rainbow water parsley

This lovely plant has pink, white, and green frilly foliage that resembles compact carrot tops. The foliage is aromatic, even edible, having a peppery, celerylike flavor that is suitable for salads and stuffings. Greg uses it to make flavored vinegars, where it imparts its pink color. Leaves grow from running stems that root quickly at the leaf nodes. Flowers are umbels of small, white, starlike blossoms that appear in summer and continue through to fall.

The plant is excellent for filtration, taking up nutrients that would otherwise contribute to green algae in the pond. It grows well along the edge of the pond, stream, or waterfall and is also suitable in a larger container water garden.

Myosotis scorpioides 'Snowflakes'

Myosotis scorpioides 'Mermaid'

Oenanthe javanica 'Flamingo', foliage detail

Oenanthe javanica 'Flamingo', at stream's edge

The pink fades in the heat of summer but returns in the fall. It makes a great ground cover in wet areas. The variegated form does not flower as profusely as its green parent, *Oenanthe javanica*, or grow as rampantly at the edge of the pond.

Situate it in sun to part shade in moist soil or water to 2 inches (5 cm) deep. Plant height is 6 inches (15 cm). Rainbow water parsley overwinters easily in colder climates and will withstand being frozen in the pond with no special care or attention. It is so hardy that it starts to grow in the ice in the spring, the dark foliage melting the ice with the sun's rays. It will also grow in the house during the winter. Zones 5–11.

Orontium aquaticum
Golden club

Orontium aquaticum is noted for its velvety, lance-shaped leaves that are dark olive-green and can reach 5–12 inches (13–30 cm) long. In late spring or early summer, the plant has unusual white, fleshy flower spikes with termi-

Orontium aquaticum

Osmunda regalis 'Purpurascens'

nal spikes of many very small yellow flowers. The overall effect is very striking. An easy-to-grow plant, it forms tight clumps, like hostas. Grow it in part sun to full shade in moist soil or water to 6 inches (15 cm) or more deep. Plant height reaches 6–10 inches (15–25 cm) with a spread of 12–18 inches (30–45 cm). Native to North America, this species varies a little over its range. The large plants in the southern United States are less hardy than their northern counterparts. Golden club overwinters well in colder climates and withstands being frozen in the pond. Red-stemmed and variegated forms are also coming onto the market. Zones 5–11.

Osmunda regalis

This tropical-looking fern can reach up to 6 feet (1.8 m) tall and wide when growing in water up to the crown in part shade. It is a truly impressive plant. Generally it grows to 3–4 feet (90–120 cm) tall and wide in sun to part shade. Foliage is a dull, army green color. The plant is great for pond edges or seasonally wet woods under bald cypress (*Taxodium*). Found in the temperate Northern Hemisphere, it grows from Canada to Central America. Fronds can be fertile or produce a terminal spore structure. Earned Royal Horticultural Society Award of Garden Merit in 1993. Zone 3 and up.

'Crispa' has wavy margins on the leaflets and grows to 2 feet (60 cm) tall and wide. Synonym *Osmunda regalis* 'Undulata'.

'Cristata' is a crested form that is very showy in the right place. Instead of coming to a terminal tip, the frond develops many tips. The plant grows to 3 feet (90 cm) tall and wide. Earned Royal Horticultural Society Award of Garden Merit in 1997.

'Gracilis' has coppery new growth and reaches 3 feet (90 cm) tall and wide. Synonym *Osmunda regalis* 'Grandiceps'.

'Purpurascens' has purplish stems and a purple cast to new growth that remains on some of the fronds through maturity. It grows to just over 3 feet (90 cm) tall and wide.

Peltandra virginica

Peltandra virginica
Bog arum, arrow arum

The foliage forms a dense clump that resembles arrowhead (*Sagittaria*) but the plant will not spread in an earthen pond, as arrowhead is prone to do. The green flowers resemble jack-in-the-pulpit (*Arisaema triphyllum*), appearing below the foliage in summer. A strong grower, bog arum is suitable for the edge of the pond and makes an excellent accent plant. Grow it in sun to part shade in moist soil or water to 6 inches (15 cm) or more deep. Plant height and spread are 24 inches (60 cm). Native to North America, bog arum can be frozen in the pond over winter. Zones 5–9.

Penthorum sedoides in flower

Peltandra species do best in 6 inches (15 cm) of water or less, but will grow, though not at their best, in water up to 4 feet (1.2 m) deep. Like many plants with a wide geographic range, bog arum has an appearance and form that can vary greatly from one population to the next. At one time, 40 species were listed, including plants that grew to 5 feet (1.5 m) with 18-inch (45-cm) wide leaves; plants with red petioles; plants with long, pointed, triangular leaves like a jester's hat; plants 12 inches (30 cm) tall with spoon-shaped foliage; plants with orange, large flowers; and plants with small, green, spotted flowers.

Penthorum sedoides
Star fruit

Much underused in the water garden, star fruit has three to five flowering wands that radiate from the center of the plant, forming a star. Each stem supports a star-shaped green flower composed of five sections, but the flowers are secondary to the fruit, which turns pink and looks like flowers. In the fall, stems and seed capsules turn pink while the foliage turns a bright golden yellow. Grow it in sun to part shade in moist soil or water to 4 inches (10 cm) deep. Plant height is 10–18 inches (25–45 cm), spread 10 inches (25 cm). This North America native withstands being frozen in the pond. Zones 4–11.

Penthorum sedoides in fruit

Petasites hybridus
flowers

Petasites hybridus
foliage

Petasites hybridus
Butter burr

Grown especially for their large, rounded foliage that looks like rhubarb (*Rheum*) and can likewise be eaten, petasites are vigorous growers that do best in large sites where they may run freely, reaching 3–4 feet (90–120 cm) high. They are excellent for naturalizing along the edge of earthen ponds and streams. In smaller water gardens, they should be kept in containers so they do not overtake their neighbors. Petasites have unusual flowers that appear early in spring before foliage has even sprouted. The flower spikes may be from 6 to 12 inches (15–30 cm) or so in height, adorned with small tufted, white, green, or even dark red flowers. The blooms last only a week or so, quickly followed by the appearance of the foliage.

Flower stalks of *Petasites hybridus* are dark red. The triangular, cupped leaves are large at 18–24 inches (45–60 cm) across and reach up to 4 feet (1.2 m) tall. Butter burr lends a bold, architectural element to the pond and is best suited for large water gardens or bogs. It prefers cooler temperatures and part to full shade. It can wilt in the heat and humidity of summer if it is not given at least afternoon shade. Overwinter plants in moist soil or in the perennial border in colder climates. Fall mulch is beneficial. If foliage gets tattered, cut it to the ground for a fresh flush. Zones 5–9.

Phyla lanceolata
Frog fruit

An ideal ground cover for the wet spot in the yard, or for a rocky margin at the edge of the pond, *Phyla lanceolata* tolerates some foot traffic and may even be mowed. It has small, lance-shaped leaves that are toothed and an even green. In the fall, foliage turns a wonderful crimson-purple color. Starting in early summer and continuing until fall, the plant is covered in tiny white flowers that resemble verbena. As they mature, they change to yellow and then pink.

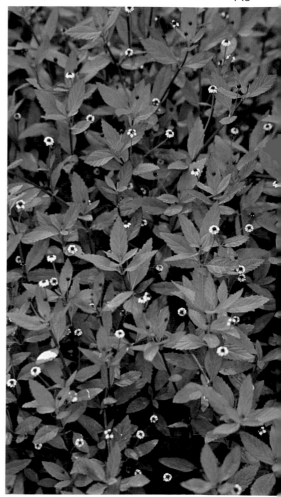

Phyla lanceolata

Frog fruit is a great plant for containers or for use as a walkable shoreline for fishing or boat access. Grow it in sun to part shade in moist soil or water to 4 inches (10 cm) deep. It reaches 2 inches (5 cm) high with a trailing spread. Plants overwinter well in cool climates without any special care or attention. Simply leave them in the pond or at the margins of the water garden. The species is native to North America. Zones 5–11.

Physostegia leptophylla

Physostegia leptophylla
Water obedient plant

This is the water-loving cousin to the perennial form of *Physostegia* commonly found in many backyard gardens. Like its land-loving relatives, the aquatic form has tubular lavender-pink flowers that appear throughout the summer. Leaves are lance-shaped and toothed.

Plant height reaches 3–4 feet (90–120 cm) and spread 2 feet (60 cm). Grow it in sun to part shade in moist soil or water to 1 inch (2.5 cm) deep. It will tolerate deep shade. The species is native to the southeastern United States. Plants overwinter well in the pond as long as their pots are submerged in the water below the freeze line. Zones 5–11.

Pontederia cordata
Blue pickerel plant

Pickerel plant is appreciated for its excellent filtration abilities. It also attracts butterflies, skippers, and hummingbirds. Dragonflies and damselflies use the upright stems as perches to shed their final larval stage and become adults. Wildfowl eat the seed, and young pickerel fish appreciate the foliage when grown in deeper water, as do other fish, frogs, and other amphibians.

Considered one of the mainstays of the water garden pond, *Pontederia cordata* has shiny, jade green, heart-shaped foliage and large spikes of blue flowers. The plant has a compact habit, growing from a rhizome that sits, like an iris, near the surface of the soil. Its native range includes North America, from Florida and Oklahoma northward to Minnesota, Nova Scotia, and Ontario, extending into South America. It is unclear whether there are two species of *Pontederia* in the United States, or only one with separate subspecies.

Grow it in sun to part shade in moist soil or water to 10 inches (25 cm) deep. Plant height is 24–30 inches (60–75 cm), spread 12–24 inches (30–60 cm). Plant hardiness varies depending heavily upon local heritage, so make sure to select a plant that has been raised for the particular climate in which it will be grown. In cold climates, plants overwinter best if the rootstock is protected from freezing. Place the rootstock well below the frost line of the pond, or remove the plant to cold, damp quarters until spring returns. Earned Royal Horticultural Society Award of Garden Merit in 1993. Zones 5–11.

'**Alba**' (white pickerel plant) has white flowers, blossoms often tinged in pink, especially at the base of the flower, and shiny, green, spoon-shaped leaves.

'**Angustifolia**' is a very upright plant, 3–5 feet (90–150 cm) tall, with icy, sky blue flowers and dark green foliage. Synonym *Pontederia cordata* 'Lanceolata'.

'**Crown Point**' has been rated as one of the best overall filtration plants in studies performed by Michael Kane at the University of Florida, Gainesville. It is more compact and bushy than the species, with flower spikes and leaves more rounded. Flowers are bright, deep blue. Plants reach 12–18 inches (30–45 cm) high and wide. Grow them in sun to part shade in moist soil or water to 18 inches (45 cm) deep. This versatile plant is well suited for reclamation and wetland sites due to its cold hardiness and its ability to filter pollutants from the water. Zones 4–11.

'**Dilatata**', sometimes sold as *Pontederia dilatata* or *P. cordata* 'Angustifolia', is a very nice plant 3–5 feet (90–150 cm) tall, spreading to 2

Pontederia cordata

Pontederia cordata 'Alba'

Potentilla palustris

Preslia cervina

feet (60 cm). Flower spikes of more than 6 inches (15 cm) display dark blue-purple blooms.

'**Pink Pons**' (pink pickerel plant) has pink-lavender flowers that are noticeably pink when placed next to their blue relatives. Grow it in sun to part shade in moist soil or water to 6 inches (15 cm) deep. Plants reach 24–30 inches (60–75 cm) high with a spread of 12–18 inches (30–45 cm).

'**Spoon River**' has very narrow, spoon- or lance-shaped leaves only 3/4 inch (18 mm) wide and up to 7 inches (18 cm) long. Flowers are intensely blue and stay erect after blooming. Grow it in sun to part shade in moist soil or water to 6 inches (15 cm) deep. Plant height is 24–30 inches (60–75 cm), spread only 6–12 inches (15–30 cm).

Potentilla palustris
Marsh cinquefoil

One of the few members of the rose family that is truly aquatic, *Potentilla palustris* has leaves that are formed of three to five leaflets, each lance-shaped and heavily toothed. A low, creeping plant up to 12 inches (30 cm) tall and wide, it roots at the edge of the pond, stream, or waterfall and then floats out across the water surface. It is rather open, not a bushy, full plant like the popular landscape shrub *P. fruticosa*. In midsummer it produces dark red flowers that resemble dainty, single roses. It is native to North America where it grows along the edges of lakes, streams, swamps, and bogs. Grow it in sun to part shade rooted in wet soil or just floating on the water surface. It does best in moving water 1–3 inches (2.5–7.5 cm) deep, such as along a stream. Zones 3–9.

Preslia cervina

This hardy mint relative is a real treasure. Very fragrant, it reaches 12–20 inches (30–50 cm) tall and has very fine leaves that look like thyme or rosemary. Grow it in full sun in moist soil to water 4 inches (10 cm) deep. It will tolerate shade. It is great along the edge of the pond or in a stream. Butterflies love it. Flowers bloom in midsummer for about three weeks in blue-purple or white. Cut it back after flowering to keep it looking nice. Zones 5–9.

RANUNCULUS

Ranunculus species are found in many parts of the world, from the tropics to the arctic. Many overwinter well in water gardens in colder climates with no special care or attention and may also be overwintered in the perennial bed with mulch for protection. Leaves can be spoon-shaped to seven-lobed and highly cut. Roots can be hairlike or tuberous. Flowers consist of five or more tepals and generally are yellow-orange to white.

Ranunculus acris
Tall buttercup

A native of Europe that has naturalized throughout the world, this buttercup grows to almost 36 inches (90 cm) high. The rounded and finely cut leaves form a mound about 24 inches (60 cm) high and 12 inches (30 cm) or so wide, with the flowers appearing higher on long, arching stems. The waxy yellow flowers appear in spring and with deadheading will continue to bloom intermittently throughout the summer. Grow the plant in sun to part shade in moist soil. It will tolerate seasonal flooding for a couple days at a time. Where cold hardy, it needs no special care to overwinter. Zones 4–9.

'**Citrinus**' is pale lemon yellow.

'**Flore Pleno**' is a double chrome-yellow. Earned Royal Horticultural Society Award of Garden Merit in 2002.

'**Sulphureus**' is golden yellow.

Ranunculus acris

Ranunculus flammula
Creeping spearwort, tongue buttercup

A native of Europe, this diminutive ranunculus grows both above and below the water surface. It has narrow leaves less than 1/4 inch (6 mm) wide and 2-1/2 inches (6 cm) long that grow in a starlike fashion from the plant's crown. Running stolons also emerge from the crown, landing a few inches away and forming a new plant. Flowers are small, bright yellow, and buttercup-like. Each stem has at least one flower. Grow the plant in sun to part shade in shallow water of 1–3 inches (2.5–7.5 cm). The plant also blooms when growing along the margin of the pond.

Ranunculus flammula

Rotala rotundifolia

Ruellia brittoniana 'Katie'

Plant height reaches 12–24 inches (30–60 cm) high, spread is 12 inches (30 cm). Zones 5–9.

'Thor' has larger flowers, is superior to the species, and is easier to grow.

Rotala rotundifolia
Pink sprite

A charming aquatic from India into Japan and Southeast Asia, *Rotala rotundifolia* has lovely red, pink, and green leaves with red stems. The small, fleshy, very rounded leaves are held close to the stem. In spring and fall, when days are short, giving less than 10 hours of sunlight, the 2-inch (5-cm) tall creeping plant is covered with pink flowers that look like miniature astilbes. It is excellent for table-top ponds and for indoor ponds, where it will flower all winter. Grow it in sun to shade in moist soil or submerged. It must be overwintered indoors as a houseplant. Zones 9–11.

RUELLIA

Though other perennial forms of *Ruellia* are often considered weeds of little ornamental significance, *Ruellia* species that grow in wet soil are sought out by water gardeners for their large, petunia-like flowers that appear all year long in the tropical climates they prefer. Foliage is usually narrow and lance-shaped, not unlike willow leaves. In colder climates, the foliage often turns dark purple once night temperatures begin to cool below 55°F (13°C). The plants do not withstand cold temperatures and must be overwintered indoors as houseplants. Zones 9–11.

Ruellia brittoniana
Water bluebell

Much favored by water gardeners, this species is constantly covered with 1- to 2-inch (2.5- to 5-cm) lavender-blue flowers. It is very easy to grow. Grow it in sun to part shade in moist soil or water to 6 inches (15 cm) deep. It reaches 2–4 feet (60–120 cm) high, sometimes more in the Deep South, and 2 feet (60 cm) wide. White forms exist, but they are weak growers.

'Chi Chi' (pink water bluebell) is just as free-flowering as other water bluebells. Foliage turns burgundy in autumn when the temperatures fall.

The plant makes a nice, bushy statement that is great with hibiscus or ludwigias.

'Katie' (dwarf water bluebell) has purple-blue, geranium-blue flowers and a dwarf, compact habit, not usually reaching more than 10 inches (25 cm) or so high and 12 inches (30 cm) wide. Instead of the usual 1–3 inches (2.5–7.5 cm) between nodes, the leaves are stacked one atop the other. Flower stems are also reduced by half, but leaves and blooms are the same size as those of the species. Grow it in sun to part shade in moist soil or water to 1 inch (2.5 cm) deep.

'Pink Katie' has pink flowers.

'Strawberries and Cream' (variegated dwarf water bluebell) has the same compact habit as 'Katie.' Its leaves are speckled in cream, pink, white, and green, becoming more green with age. Flowers are a soft purplish blue.

Ruellia squarrosa 'Alba'
White water bluebell

This form has crepe-paper white flowers. The leaf shape is a little different—rounded rather than pointed and willowy. Grow it in sun to part shade in moist soil or water to 6 inches (15 cm) deep. Plant height is 2–4 feet (60–120 cm), spread 2 feet (60 cm). This cultivar is often sold as *Ruellia brittoniana* 'Alba', because the species look so similar except for the leaves.

Ruellia squarrosa 'Alba'

*Rumex
orbiculatus*

*Sagittaria
'Bloomin' Baby'*

Rumex orbiculatus
Water dock, great water dock

A much-underused and unnoticed marginal plant, *Rumex orbiculatus* has shiny, dark green, lance-shaped leaves that are about 2 inches (5 cm) wide and 4 inches (10 cm) long. In the summer, green flower heads appear as drooping plumes, turning to brown and taking on a graceful, almost feathery appearance. Grow it in sun to part shade in moist soil or water to 6 inches (15 cm) deep. Plant height reaches 36 inches (90 cm), spread is 24 inches (60 cm). Native to temperate regions, including North America, this cold- and frost-tolerant water plant requires no special care or maintenance to survive cold winters. Zones 5–11.

SAGITTARIA
Arrowhead

Named for its arrow shaped leaves held atop long stems that rise from a central base, *Sagittaria* is highly ornamental at the edge of the pond and is very easy to grow. It contributes to the water garden landscape with both its clean, geometric foliage and its delicate white flowers. Plants are attractive when mixed with pontederias or planted near hibiscus and grasses like *Scirpus*.

In the fall, arrowhead develops underground tubers before the mother plant dies. These small tubers, called turions, will sprout and grow the coming spring. Water gardeners often believe that their arrowhead plant has died, only to find that it has set turions at the bottom of the pot. Finding the turions early each spring and repotting them will continue the arrowhead heritage in the pond for years to come. When potting up turions, plant them well toward the bottom of the pot. Fill the pot one-fourth full with soil, place the turions on the soil, then fill the pot with soil. Each turion will elongate and place a new plantlet at the top of the soil.

Cold-tolerant *Sagittaria* species are native to much of North America, with numerous species growing in localized areas or parts of the continent. Other species are native to tropical regions of Central and South America, and the odd plant occurs here or there in the rest of the world.

Sagittaria 'Bloomin' Baby'

A dwarf, extremely free-flowering arrowhead that is most likely a form of *Sagittaria cuneata*, 'Bloomin' Baby' emerges earlier than other arrowheads and often starts to bloom when it is only 3 inches (7.5 cm) tall. Grow it in sun to part shade in moist soil or water to 2 inches (5 cm) deep. Although it will grow in water 24 inches (60 cm) deep, it will only send up floating foliage; it will not bloom. Plant height reaches 3–10 inches (7.5–25 cm) tall with a running spread. Zones 5–11.

Sagittaria lancifolia
White swan

This tender species has tall lance-shaped leaves that arch outward from their irislike rhizome. The overall effect creates the impression of the wings of a swan. The single white flowers appear throughout the summer on long stems that also arch up and outward, complementing the sway of the foliage. Grow it in sun to part shade in moist soil or water to 10 inches (25 cm) deep.

Sagittaria lancifolia

Plant height is 1–4 feet (30–120 cm), spread is 1–2 feet (30–60 cm). Zones 8–11.

Forma ruminoides (red swan) is similar to the species except that the base of each leaf stem is brushed in bright red. This can vary from supplier, from lightly blushed to almost black to a spotted or striped pattern.

Sagittaria latifolia

The standard arrowhead, *Sagittaria latifolia*, is widely distributed across North America and through Central and South America. It sports the characteristic arrow-shaped leaves and single, clear white flowers. Leaves may grow submerged, becoming long and tapered, closely resembling *Vallisneria*. This is a favorite food of muskrats. Often selected as a wetland reclamation plant, this species self-seeds readily and takes up water quickly. It can form large colonies that shade out other aquatics like *Myosotis*, so plant wisely. Grow it in sun to part shade in moist soil or water to 6 inches (15 cm) or more deep. Plant height is 12–20 inches (30–50 cm) with a running spread. Zones 3–11.

Because of its large range, the species varies greatly, from flowering above the foliage to below, from having narrow bladeless leaves to very narrow arrow-shaped leaves to broad and rounded arrow-shaped leaves. Some species have hair on the foliage, others have red or brown spotting on either juvenile or mature foliage. Some species have a red cast to new growth. Some have branched flower stalks. Tuber size varies as does hardiness, based on provenance of original plant material. Some selections that take advantage of these variations have been made and named, but a lot of room remains for interesting selections in this species.

'**Brevifolia**' (needle-leaf arrowhead) has extremely narrow leaves that are sharply pointed at each of their three corners. It has a more delicate and angular appearance than the species, but is just as easy to care for. Its very vertical foliage is perfect for a more grassy or Eastern look.

'**Flore Pleno**' displays very double, ruffled, frilly flowers. The earlier flowers on small plants tend to be not as showy but look like wet popcorn.

'**Leopard Spot**' has prominent brown-purple spots on rounded arrow-shaped foliage and grows to 24 inches (60 cm) high and wide.

Sagittaria montevidensis
Aztec arrowhead

This tropical beauty has giant foliage that is deeply veined and of a stronger texture than other arrowheads. Flowers are abundant, with single white petals marked with a red dot and yellow centers. Grow it in sun to part shade in

Sagittaria latifolia

Sagittaria latifolia 'Brevifolia'

Sagittaria montevidensis

Samolus parviflorus

Sarracenia purpurea

moist soil or water to 5 inches (13 cm) deep. Plant height is 2–4 feet (60–120 cm), spread 3 feet (90 cm). In warmer climates, some plants produce a cormlike overwintering structure. This is truly an annual species, however, producing copious amounts of seed rather than tubers. It is native from South America to South Dakota. Zones 8–11.

Samolus parviflorus
Water alyssum

Leaves of this dainty water plant grow in basal rosettes that form a neat clump. Flowers rise a few inches above the foliage in summer and consist of white sprays of small, fine-textured blooms. Water alyssum is good for a ground cover or as an accent plant near the edge of the pond. It is also good for containers. Grow it in sun to part shade in moist soil to submerged. Plant height is 6–12 inches (15–30 cm), spread 6 inches (15 cm). Samolus species are found in many parts of the world, mainly in the Southern Hemisphere. This species can overwinter in the pond. Zone 5.

SARRACENIA
Pitcher plant

Sarracenias make a great addition in neutral to acidic water gardens. They are like no other water plant, with alien-looking, pitcher-shaped leaves and flowers like Japanese processional lanterns. They are very effective at trapping and killing insects. Greg has found them so full of mosquitoes that he had to scoop them out to keep the pitchers from being damaged. Depending on species or selection, plant height is 6–24 inches (15–60 cm), spread 6 inches (15 cm). Flower color ranges from white to yellow, red, or pink in summer. Grow them in sun to part shade in moist soil or water to 1 inch (2.5 cm) deep. Plant in live sphagnum for best results. Some growers have success with a mix of sand and peat moss. Zone 7.

Sarracenia ×catesbyi is copper-colored, growing to 12 inches (60 cm) high and wide. Earned Royal Horticultural Society Award of Garden Merit in 1993.

Sarracenia flava

Sarracenia 'Dixie Lace' has new pitchers emerging all season and reaching 18 inches (45 cm) in a coppery butterscotch color with red veins.

Sarracenia flava has yellow pitchers to 24 inches (60 cm). Earned Royal Horticultural Society Award of Garden Merit in 1993.

Sarracenia 'Flies Demise' has dusty orange and red pitchers to 10 inches (25 cm) tall.

Sarracenia 'Ladies in Waiting' has many red pitchers up to 24 inches (60 cm) tall with white dots.

Sarracenia leucophylla has white pitchers to 18 inches (45 cm). 'Turnock' has double, red-yellow flowers on standard pitchers.

Sarracenia 'Mardi Gras' has many large cobra hoods of white, green, and red on 12-inch (30-cm) plants.

Sarracenia purpurea is the hardiest pitcher plant at Zone 3. It is common on moss and willow islands in the lakes of northern Minnesota. 'Blood Vessel' is a 12-inch (30-cm) selection with deep red veins.

SAURURUS

Saururus species, found in North America and in Southeast Asia, are known for their heart-shaped leaves that appear alternately on tall stems growing from creeping rhizomes. The plant forms dense colonies of upright stems topped with drooping spikes of white flowers. Both the flowers and the stems are aromatic, having a pleasant fragrance similar to vanilla or ginger. Plants will withstand a frost but cannot tolerate being frozen in the pond. Move the underground rhizomes so that they will not freeze during the winter. Zones 4–11.

Saururus cernuus
Lizard tail

Lizard tail is well suited to the water garden landscape, providing a taller backdrop for smaller plants. It is useful because its white flow-ers bloom for a long period, usually for about a month in early summer, and it returns year after year. Plants are somewhat variable. Grow it in sun to part shade in moist soil or water to 6 inches (15 cm) deep. Plant height reaches 12–36 inches (30–90 cm) with a running spread. The plant tolerates seasonal flooding and grows well along streams or in shady wetlands. It is also good for detention ponds with a wet corner.

Var. **ruminoides** (red-stemmed lizard tail) has red stems that make the plant even more attrac-tive than the standard species.

Saururus chinensis
Chinese lizard tail

An extremely attractive pondside plant, Chinese lizard tail has a white splotch on the topmost leaves, like bracts on a poinsettia, that make the plant ornamental even when it is not in flower.

Saururus cernuus

Saururus chinensis

Grow it in sun to part shade in moist soil or water to 6 inches (15 cm) deep. Plants reach 18–36 inches (45–90 cm) with a running spread. Height is greatly affected by exposure. Greg has seen plants 40 inches (100 cm) tall in shade and 12 inches (30 cm) in full sun.

'Oregon Gold', an all-gold selection, is very showy but slow to grow.

Schoenoplectus tabernaemontani
Soft rush

Graceful, green cylinders of foliage have large, brown pendulous flowers. Combined with *Pontederia* or *Peltandra*, this species is a knockout in the landscape. It has a wide distribution. Grow it in sun to part shade in moist soil or water to 10 inches (25 cm) deep. Plant height is 2–6 feet (60–180 cm), with a running spread. Synonym *Scirpus validus*. Zones 3–11.

'Golden Spears' is very showy with yellow stems in spring that turn green in summer.

SCIRPUS
Bulrush

Scirpus species can be found in many parts of the world, including North America. They usually have foliage that is thin, narrow, and tall. Flowers are brown clubs or plumes that appear in mid to late summer. Many species are cold tolerant and will survive a winter freeze as long as they remain in the pond. Rushes are excellent for shoreline stabilization in a natural pond or stream. They provide important cover for wildlife, including birds and amphibians, as well as nesting grounds for wildlife and fishes.

Scirpus albescens
White rush

The excellent, upright habit of this marginal makes a good accent in the pond The cylindrical foliage has strong white vertical stripes in spring, but these markings are not so pronounced in summer when the weather turns warm and

Schoenoplectus tabernaemontani

Scirpus albescens

muggy. Grow it in sun to part shade in moist soil or water to 3 inches (7.5 cm) deep. It will grow in water 24 inches (60 cm) deep but will be a much less dense, more open stand. Plants reach 4–6 feet (1.2–1.8 m) high with a running spread. Zones 5–9.

Scirpus cyperinus
Woolly rush

Distinguished by its fluffy, silken tassels of tawny brown that appear at the ends of stiff, dark green foliage, woolly rush forms a dense clump 4 feet (1.2 m) high and half as wide. Unlike other

Scirpus cyperinus

Scirpus species, it does not run. It looks more like a *Cyperus* species than a *Scirpus*. Grow it in sun to part shade in moist soil or water to 4 inches (10 cm) deep. Zones 3–9.

Sium suave
Water parsnip

The submerged leaves of water parsnip are very finely cut, more so even than the leaves of carrots. As they emerge above the water they become coarser until they look like parsnip foliage, or Italian parsley if crowded. The plant grows from a central stalk that shoots forth umbels of starry white flowers in summer through fall. One stalk, if planted alone, forms almost a shrub. The species is native to temperate regions of North America. Grow it in sun to part shade in moist soil or water to 6 inches (15 cm) deep. Plants reach 3–5 feet (90–150 cm) high with a spread of 2–3 feet (60–90 cm). They overwinter well in the pond with no special care or protection. Water parsnip looks great with *Pontederia* or *Thalia*, giving a baby's breath effect. It should be used more. Zones 4–11.

SPARGANIUM
Burr reed

Daylily-like foliage grows submerged in deep water or emerged in shallow. Most emerged foliage is just over 24 inches (60 cm) tall. Each plant spreads to only 4–6 inches (10–15 cm), but they form colonies like cattails (*Typha*). Flowers are little white balls on zigzag stems, some branched, some not. Sweetly scented and attractive to skipper butterflies, they bloom all summer, followed by spiny-looking balls of fruit. Leaves are a bright, translucent celery green, and fall color

Sium suave

Sparganium

is banana yellow with a hint of pumpkin. These very showy plants are fairly open growing and do not crowd out other plants.

Fourteen species are native throughout the Northern Hemisphere and into Australasia. Most of the North American species look very similar when emerged. All are useful in the water garden, either in containers or in drifts. Look for *Sparganium americanum*, *S. androcladum*, *S. emersum*, *S. eurycarpum*, *S. fluctuans*, *S. glomeratum*, and *S. natans*. The mature seed of these species is about the only way to tell them apart. All are very adaptable. Corms can be overwintered. Zones 2–10.

Stachys palustris
Marsh betony
A hardy and reliable water plant native to North America, marsh betony has thick spikes of pink or purple flowers in summer. Leaves resemble those of *Monarda* and are hairy. In the fall, foliage takes on a maroon or yellow color. Grow it in moist soil, where its running spread may be invasive, or in water as deep as 5 inches (13 cm). Plant height reaches 6–24 inches (15–60 cm). Plants overwinter in cold climates with no special care or protection, as long as their pots remain submerged in the water. Zones 4–8.

Symplocarpus foetidus
American skunk cabbage
Very similar in appearance to yellow and white skunk cabbage (*Lysichiton*), American skunk cabbage has large, leathery, and lance- to spade-shaped leaves. Springtime flowers are smaller than those of other skunk cabbages, with a pointed, shell-like spathe of dark red, brown, green, or speckled enclosing a small, fleshy

Stachys palustris

Symplocarpus foetidus

flower spike. Native to North America, the species grows in the eastern and midwestern parts of the continent, as well as in temperate eastern Asia and Japan. Grow it in part shade in moist soil or water to 3 inches (7.5 cm) deep. Plants reach 36 inches (90 cm) high and wide. Asian forms of the species are shorter, reaching 12–18 inches (30–45 cm), with very red, shiny flowers. American skunk cabbage overwinters in colder climates without special protection; the heat of its growth in spring actually melts the snow around it. A variegated form also exists. Zones 3–9.

THALIA

Native to tropical regions of the Americas, *Thalia* species are grown primarily for their striking, lush foliage. Leaves are ovate to lance-shaped and can become rather large, up to 24 inches (60 cm) across at their widest, and often more than 36 inches (90 cm) long. Flowers are unusual silvery purple beads that droop from long, arching stems.

Thalia dealbata
Purple thalia

Thalia dealbata is a hardy species, overwintering in colder climates with no special protection. The purple flowers bloom in late summer. The foliage looks very tropical and has a slight powdery blue color. "Blue Cup-leafed Form" is a selection with blue leaves that are more cup-shaped than those of the species. "Broad-leafed Form" has leaves that are flat and more triangular in shape. Grow these plants in sun to part shade in moist soil or water to 6 inches (15 cm) deep. They reach a height of 2–6 feet (60–180 cm) with a spread of 2 feet (60 cm). Zone 5.

Thalia dealbata

Thalia geniculata

Typha angustifolia

Typha latifolia 'Variegata'

Typha
laxmannii

Thalia geniculata
Alligator flag
The common name of this thalia derives from its usefulness in "flagging" the presence of an alligator; as the gator swims through a glade, it rustles the plant, causing the leaves to swing back and forth. Foliage is more yellow-green than that of *Thalia dealbata*, and the late-summer flowers are silvery blue. Grow it in sun to part shade in moist soil or water to 10 inches (25 cm) deep. Plants reach 2–9 feet (60–280 cm) high with a spread of 2–6 feet (60–180 cm) This is a more tender species that will not survive a winter frost. Bring it indoors to spend the winter. Zones 9–11.

Forma ruminoides (red-stemmed alligator flag) has stems streaked in red and sometimes solid red, giving it an even greater accent value in the pond. This form grows slightly larger than the standard species, reaching 2–10 feet (60–300 cm) high and 2–6 feet (60–180 cm) wide.

TYPHA
Cattail
Cattail foliage is narrow, anywhere from 1/2 to 2 inches (12–25 mm) wide, depending upon the species. Height can range from 6 inches (15 cm) to more than 12 feet (3.6 m) tall. Leaves are generally flat on one side and more rounded on the other. Flowers are long catkins that turn brown as they mature, releasing downy seeds that float away on the breeze. Cattails grow in freshwater marshes and colonize wide areas with their stiff, running rhizomes. They tolerate water over their crown and provide important habitat for fish and amphibians. Their foliage serves as a nesting source for many species of wild birds, and their roots are often eaten by muskrats. Leaves and roots have also had their place as a source of food for humans—the rootstock can be ground into flour, and the new shoots may be boiled and eaten as a vegetable. Cattails overwinter

well in cooler water and withstand freezing temperatures. Native to many parts of the world, these species grow wild in North America, from Newfoundland to Alaska and southward into Mexico.

Typha angustifolia
Graceful cattail
More narrow than the foliage of common cattail (*Typha latifolia*), the foliage of graceful cattail arches and sways gracefully in the breeze. The plant is very elegant and suitable for most ponds and large container water gardens. The very thin catkins make attractive additions to floral arrangements. Grow the plant in sun to part shade in moist soil or water to 12 inches (30 cm) deep. Plant height is 4–6 feet (1.2–1.8 m). Zones 3–11.

Typha latifolia
A bold vertical accent in any pond, this cattail is the one commonly seen growing in ditches and in wetlands. It is excellent for water filtration and should not be dismissed for its value in the water garden landscape. Grow it in sun to part shade in moist soil or water to 12 inches (30 cm) deep. Plant height reaches 7 feet (2.1 m) tall. Zones 3–11.

'Variegata' (variegated cattail) has bold, clean, bright green and white longitudinal stripes. An elegant addition to any pond, it does not grow as readily as other cattails and does not appreciate being transplanted. Plant height is 5–6 feet (1.5–1.8 m). Zones 4–11.

Typha laxmannii
Dwarf cattail
Ideal for small ponds and container water gardens, dwarf cattail has very narrow foliage and small catkins. It is not as heat tolerant as other cattails. Grow it in sun to part shade in moist soil or water to just 4 inches (10 cm) deep. Plant height is only about 36 inches (90 cm). Zones 3–10.

Typha minima, catkins

Typha minima, in winter

Typha minima
Miniature cattail

Perfect for the very small pond or container garden, this miniature species has petite, round catkins on petite, vertical plants. Foliage is often an attractive blue-green color. Grow the plant in sun to part shade in moist soil or water to 3 inches (7.5 cm) deep. Plant height is just 12–18 inches (30–45 cm). Zones 3–9.

VERONICA

Veronica species are native to northern temperate regions. Of the 250 species in the genus, about 10 are aquatic. The low creeping or bushy plants are covered in blue flowers. Some species exhibit burgundy fall color. The foliage varies dramatically among the species, from round to stringy, but the flowers are generally the same deep to pale blue. Plants overwinter well in colder climates with no special protection. They can simply remain in the pond throughout the winter. Zones 5–9.

Veronica americana
American brooklime

This North American native has lance-shaped leaves that are slightly toothed. Flowers are tubular and light blue, appearing on spikes that grow from the leaf axils. Very free-flowering in spring and early summer, American brooklime has an upright, bushy habit and does not run into or interfere with its neighbors. It is suitable for the edge of the pond or bog garden, or in a table-top pond. Although it reproduces readily from seed, it is never a pest. It may be annual in some ponds, but new seedlings are up and ready by fall for overwintering in the pond. Situate the plant in sun to part shade in moist soil or water to 3 inches (7.5 cm) deep. Plant height is 4–12 inches (10–30 cm), spread 10–12 inches (25–30 cm). Zones 5–9.

Veronica beccabunga
European brooklime

Native to Europe, this species has a shorter, more creeping habit than its American coun-

Veronica americana

Veronica beccabunga

Wedelia trilobata

terpart. Foliage is rounded and slightly toothed, shiny, and fleshy. It displays great fall color of intense crimson. Flowers are bright blue, appearing at the leaf axils in spring to summer. A delightful addition to the pond, European brooklime has a tendency to run and needs some pruning to restrain its presence. It is particularly well suited for a small tub garden or table-top pond. Grow it in sun to part shade in moist soil or water to 3 inches (7.5 cm) deep. Plant height is 4 inches (10 cm), spread is 12 inches (30 cm). Zones 5–9.

Wedelia trilobata
Golden water zinnia
A trailing plant with yellow zinnia-like flowers in summer, this tropical is excellent in waterfalls or on the pond edge. A variegated form is available with yellow-splashed foliage; it is a nice addition, especially in shade, but be vigilant to remove any all-green shoots. Grow golden water zinnia in sun to shade in moist soil or water to 1 inch (2.5 cm) deep. It also tolerates drought. Plant height reaches 6 inches (15 cm). Plants require protection during winter. Bring them inside and treat them as houseplants. Zones 9–11.

XYRIS
Yellow-eyed grass

The acid-requiring plants in the genus *Xyris* have grassy or irislike foliage at the base and clublike flower heads that rise above the foliage. Bright yellow, three-petaled flowers are borne on these clubs all summer long. Foliage is often tinged with red or purple. Seeds look like little hemlock cones. Of the 250 species found throughout the world, 10 to 15 species are native to the United States. The major difference between the species listed here are size and hardiness. They grow 4–24 inches (10–60 cm) tall and wide, depending on species, in full sun to shade in moist soil or water to 4 inches (10 cm) deep. They are great in combination with *Sarracenia*. More should be done in adding them to the waterscape. They need no special care to overwinter where hardy. Otherwise, bring indoors and treat as houseplants.

Xyris difformis has flowers 2/3 inch (16 mm) in diameter. They continue all summer. The foliage is very grassy. Plant height is 2–18 inches (30–45 cm). Zone 5 and up.

Xyris fimbriata has large 1/2-inch (12-mm) flowers on plants that grow up to 24 inches (60 cm) tall. Leaves are narrower at 1/2 inch (12 mm) wide, forming clumps 24 inches (60 cm) across. Greg has observed specimens in the wild with 20 stems and almost red foliage and deep red stems. The species is very showy with *Sarracenia flava* or any of the new red-leafed cultivars. Zone 8 and up.

Xyris montana has flowers 1/3–1/2 inch (8–12 mm) in diameter on plants that grow 12 inches (60 cm) tall. Zone 4 and up.

Xyris torta has wider foliage, like *X. fimbriata*, but it is twisted. Flowers are up to 1/2 inch (12 mm) in diameter. Zone 4 and up.

Zantedeschia aethiopica
Calla lily

One of six species in the genus, all native to South Africa, *Zantedeschia aethiopica* is the classic large, white calla lily. Great as a specimen or in a stand, it grows to 4 feet (1.2 m) high and wide. Bring plants indoors for the winter, letting them dry in the pot until one month before setting them out; then water them and place them in a sunny window. Much breeding has been done in the genus to create brilliant hybrids that need to be explored for the water garden. Depending on the selection, foliage is arrow-shaped to lanceolate, green or dotted with white. One selection with yellow-streaked foliage is interesting as a specimen but too much en masse. Flower color ranges from white to almost black-red, including yellows, pinks, and reds. There are no blues. All calla lilies like very moist to wet soils but no water over the crown. Earned Royal Horticultural Society Award of Garden Merit in 1993. Zone 6 or 7, depending on the selection and the protection given it.

Xyris

'Apple Court Babe' is a dwarf at 12 inches (60 cm) tall. It has numerous 2- to 4-inch (5- to 10-cm) flowers and is hardier than other selections.

'Crowborough' has white flowers and grows 18–24 inches (45–60 cm) tall. This British selection is not as hardy as 'Apple Court Babe'. Earned Royal Horticultural Society Award of Garden Merit in 1997.

'Crowborough Variegated' has yellow-splashed foliage that is very unstable and easily reverts. The plant grows 18 inches (45 cm) tall and 12 inches (30 cm) wide.

'Green Goddess' has white flowers with green tips and grows to 4 feet (1.2 m) tall. Earned Royal Horticultural Society Award of Garden Merit in 1993.

'Little Gem' has creamy white flowers and reaches 1 foot (30 cm) tall.

'Whipped Cream', also with white flowers, has heavily spotted foliage and grows 3 feet (90 cm) tall.

'White Giant' has white flowers and white-spotted foliage. Plants grow 6-1/2 feet (2 m) tall.

Zephyranthes candida
Rain lily

Native to the United States and Mexico, *Zephyranthes* species go dormant in the dry season and grow and flower in the wet season. They can grow year-round in wet sites but tend to flower better if they get a dry period. All are 3–10 inches (7.5–25 cm) tall with grassy foliage. The six-petaled flowers are 1–3 inches (2.5–7.5 cm) across in white, yellow, or pink. They grow in full sun to part shade in moist soil or water to

Zantedeschia aethiopica

Zantedeschia aethiopica 'Crowborough Variegated'

3 inches (7.5 cm) deep. These tender perennial bulbs can be overwintered indoors. Just do not water them until returning them to the pond in the spring. Zone 8 and up.

Zephyranthes candida has white flowers with a crocuslike shape, betraying their common name of water crocus. It has survived in Greg's Zone 5 or 6 garden for years.

Zephyranthes candida

Zizania aquatica
Wild rice

Zizania aquatica is a tall, stately plant that is much underused in the water garden landscape. Plumes appear in midsummer and continue throughout the fall, giving a very exotic appearance to the pond. Very easy to grow, this species has a tendency to run by its underground rhizomes. It is best suited to a large pot, even in the earth-bottom pond. It grows in full sun, producing floating foliage with 24- to 36-inch (60- to 90-cm) flower stalks above the water in water deeper than 36 inches (90 cm). In shallower water of 12 inches (30 cm) deep or less, plants can grow to 7 feet (2.1 m) or more. Flower panicles are large, generally 1–2 feet (30–60 cm) long and 1 foot (30 cm) wide. The species is native to North America, from Nova Scotia to Manitoba, into Minnesota, Nebraska, and Texas. It grows best where there is some moving water, and in the wild generally will not grow in areas where water is stagnant. Zone 5.

Zizania aquatica

IRISES

Resilient and remarkably pest-free, waterside irises reward the gardener with years of early summer flowers. True water irises grow best with water over their crown throughout the year, even in fall and winter. These include *Iris fulva*, *I. laevigata*, *I. versicolor*, *I. virginica*, and the Louisiana irises. Water-tolerant irises grow best with wet soils for some of the growing season but in most climates prefer drier conditions for the remainder of the year. These include *I. ensata* and the Siberian irises.

Irises bloom from late spring to midsummer, depending on the species or cultivar. A few irises rebloom later in the season.

Plant Parts and Habit

Like hardy waterlilies, the irises described here grow from underground swollen stems called rhizomes. Their root system is extensive. The sword-shaped leaves are upright growing and range from a solid green to various variegations of white or yellow, depending on the species and cultivar. The flowers also are upright growing and borne on stems above the leaves. Flower colors range from white to deep blue, with purple and lavender hues, reds, yellows, browns, and greens. Some flowers are deeply veined or heavily marked with a yellow glow toward the center of the petals. All the flowers have six petals. The three upper ones are known as the standards, the three lower ones as the falls.

Landscape Uses

Irises are central landscape plants for the water garden. The flowers generally rise above the leaves of the plant, and often they appear to be floating on air. From a distance, they could easily be mistaken for brightly colored butterflies.

The substantial root systems of many irises often make them excellent for holding back soil erosion along the banks of natural ponds and streams. Some irises tolerate seasonal drought as well as seasonal flooding, thus earning them a place in detention or retention areas in the larger, corporate landscape. Even a ditch or a wet spot in the homeowner's backyard is perfectly suited to many moisture-loving *Iris* species.

Water garden irises blend well with many other pondside plants, especially those that grow closer to the water surface and have delicate foliage. *Iris* leaves also serve to shade smaller inhabitants, like marsh marigold (*Caltha*), which shuns the heat of the summer sun.

Optimal Growing Conditions

Sun: At least six hours of sun, with morning sun preferable to afternoon sun.
Wind tolerance: Gentle breezes ok.
Water depth: Moist soil to water a few inches over the crown.
Soil and water chemistry: Clay soil with little organic matter, from acidic to alkaline depending on the plant.
Temperature: Warm water at least 65°F (18°C).
Salt tolerance: None.

Seasonal Care

Water irises are dependent upon seasonal changes in day length and water or soil temperature to induce them to go dormant in the winter and to prompt them to start growing again in the spring.

Spring: Bring potted *water irises* up near the surface of the pond where the water is warmer. Remove mulch and debris from *water-tolerant irises* planted in soil near the edge of the pond; this allows the sun's rays to warm the plant and its soil environment.
Summer: Begin fertilizing irises when the water temperature reaches 65°F (18°C). Continue to fertilize at one-month intervals through the season. Remove old flowers and unsightly foliage to improve plant appearance.

Green- and white-striped *Iris laevigata* 'Variegata' grows at the edge of water surrounded by the three-lobed leaves of *Menyanthes* in the foreground, the heart-shaped foliage of *Houttuynia cordata* 'Flore Pleno' at the left, narrow-leaved *Acorus gramineus* at the right, and golden *Carex elata* 'Knightshayes' in the background.

Fall: Withhold fertilizer about a month before the last frost-free date, or, in frost-free climates, withhold fertilizer when plants begin to stop growing new foliage and older leaves begin to wither and turn brown. Trim the leaves back to just an inch (2.5 cm) or so above the crown of the plant.

Winter: Submerge potted *water irises* to a depth in the pond where they will not freeze. *Water-tolerant irises* will survive cold winters in the moist soil of a bog as long as the crown of the plant is not covered, but they will not survive when grown in a pond. Remove potted water tolerant irises from the pond, set them in a temporary hole in an open spot of the perennial border, and mulch them heavily. Where the temperature stays above 25°F (-4°C), remove potted water-tolerant irises from the pond and place them a pan filled with water 1–4 inches (2.5–10 cm) deep, making sure to keep the plant crown above the water level.

Planting

Irises grow best in wide, shallow pots. Plant the rhizome toward the edge of the pot with the growing tip pointing toward the center. Spread out the roots on a mound of soil, then add soil over the rhizome and growing tip. The rhizome should be covered by soil with the growing tip just barely below the soil surface.

When water-tolerant irises outgrow their living quarters, they have a tendency to push against the edge of the pot and then "jump" out of the pot entirely. Finding a pot that is at least a foot (30 cm) in diameter will help keep this from happening too frequently. Louisiana irises are such exuberant growers that they are especially prone to running and easily jump from their pots in a single season. Grow them in a large, shallow tray to avoid replanting them in midseason.

The best time to plant or transplant an iris is immediately after it has finished flowering, when it is actively growing new roots. Although other sources recommend planting irises in late summer or early fall, we in our midwestern (Zone 5) climate have suffered severe losses through the winter with irises planted out at this time. In such colder climates, if transplanting must wait

until later in the summer, it is imperative that the plants be mulched heavily to withstand the winter cold.

Fall transplanting is appropriate in warmer climates where the irises will not be exposed to a winter of freezing temperatures and blowing winds. In such climates, water irises that are planted or transplanted just after flowering will have to endure not only transplant shock, but also the long, hot, muggy weather of summer. Many irises cannot survive such a double punch and succumb before the new season has begun.

Iris ensata
Japanese iris

Iris ensata, once known as *I. kaempferi*, grows naturally in Japan and on the Asian continent and has been widely cultivated in Asia, the United States, and the United Kingdom. It generally grows to about 24–36 inches (60–90 cm) high, sometimes taller, with thin, upright foliage. Flowers are usually held well above the foliage and may be single, double, or multipetaled. Colors range from deep, velvety purple through to the cleanest white. The blossoms are generally flat, with most of the petals hanging downward. In the water garden, they are exquisite, with midsummer flowers usually 6 inches (15 cm) or more in diameter. *Iris ensata* earned the Royal Horticultural Society Award of Garden Merit in 1994.

Japanese irises prefer wet soils in the spring and summer, and will tolerate up to 2–3 inches (5–7.5 cm) of water over the crown during these times of year. They do not survive seasonal flooding of a few feet of water over the crown in spring or summer. They should not be left in the water over the winter, especially in colder climates. Ice formation around the crown of the plant often leads to its demise, and it will not reappear the following spring. The safest practice is to follow the time-honored rule that Japanese irises should be removed from the pond and placed in a cool, dark place for the winter. Mulching them over in the perennial border is an ideal solution. In warmer climates with more temperate winters, *Iris ensata* is more likely to flourish even if it remains in the pond for the winter.

'Crown Imperial' is a white double with rolling, ruffled petals. Numerous blue veins radiate out from a small blue halo surrounding the yellow signal. The crowning glory of the flower is the centerpiece of erect, multiple, imperial blue styles with large matching blue crests. The plant forms one to two branches and reaches 36–40 inches (90–100 cm) tall. It blooms in midseason.

'Dark Lightning' is a very dark blue-violet with a lightning white halo surrounding the yellow signal and sparkling white rays that strike only halfway down the falls.

'Dragon Mane' is a large, dramatic, multipetaled white with red-violet veins and purple styles.

'Edged Delight' is white with a delightful blue rim around the standards.

'Epimethius' is wine red with splashes, speckles, and streaks of white, lavender, and lilac. It grows to 40 inches (100 cm) tall and blooms in mid to late season.

'Espata' is a lightly ruffled dark plum-violet with lighter shoulders and edges of rose-violet. A dark blue-violet halo surrounds the yellow signal. White to light violet sanded styles hold large and flared violet crests. The plant is very vigorous and has performed well in a wide range of soils.

'Fond Kiss' has large warm white flowers with a pink flush on the falls. It grows to 33 inches (83 cm) tall and blooms in midseason.

'Frosted Plum' is white with a purple halo and veins, plum-purple styles, and white wire rims.

'Hue and Cry' is purple with white veins, white style arms, and yellow signals. Earned

Iris ensata 'Hue and Cry'

Iris ensata 'Southern Son'

Royal Horticultural Society Award of Garden Merit in 1996.

'**Muffington**' is pearl white with a plum halo and veining out to white rims. Styles are purple.

'**Peak of Pink**' is a near white-pink with sharp, true pink styles and style crests.

'**Pinkerton**' is the truest pink. It has darker pink veins and creamy pink styles with pink crests. It forms two or three branches.

'**Pooh Bah**' is bright red-violet with white rays. Styles are white with red-violet crests.

'**Rafferty**' is lavender-pink with stamens that produce petaloids to full extra petals.

'**Rosewater**' is rose-violet with a blue halo and violet styles. Its flaring form blooms in late season.

'**Ruby Star**' is bright red with a white star halo. Styles are white with red crests.

'**Sapphire Crown**' is white with a blue-violet halo and veins, and purple style arms.

'**Shinto Rings**' has bright white flowers with 1/2-inch (12-mm) ring edges of rose to red-violet. Arching creamy white styles have white crests with just a fringe edge of rose-violet. The large, horizontal blooms are displayed on top of the foliage. The plant grows to 32–36 inches (80–90 cm) tall with one branch and blooms in midseason.

'**Silver Band**' has wine red blooms on cream-variegated foliage.

'**Southern Son**' is bright blue-purple with yellow signals. Earned Royal Horticultural Society Award of Garden Merit in 1995.

Iris fulva
Copper iris, red flag

Iris fulva is native to the central and southern United States east of the Mississippi River, ranging from Illinois and Missouri southward to Georgia and Louisiana. It is a smaller iris in both plant and flower, growing to 12 inches (30 cm) or so in height. Its slender leaves droop slightly at the tips, giving the plant a graceful air. The falls and standards of the 3-inch (7.5-cm) flower also hang downward, causing the blooms to resemble miniature, copper-colored *I. laevigata*

or *I. ensata*. Earned Royal Horticultural Society Award of Garden Merit in 2004.

Iris fulva grows well in full sun or part shade. It usually flowers in early summer, about the same time as other Louisiana irises, for which it is one of the parents. Preferred water depth is generally from evenly moist soil to water about 3 inches (7.5 cm) over the crown of the plant. It is the most water-tolerant iris. The plant performs well in sites that dry out during the summer and tolerates seasonal flooding.

Copper irises easily survive a winter freeze, provided they remain in the pond water. In very warm climates, the plant should be permitted to

Iris fulva

Iris fulva 'Marvell Gold'

spend some time in dormancy—cease fertilizing and allow it to dry out to just damp. No hard-and-fast rules determine the required degree of dormancy—it depends largely upon the cultivar. Zones 5–11.

'Marvell Gold' has golden yellow flowers that glow in the water garden.

Iris laevigata
Rabbit ear iris

Originating in eastern Asia, *Iris laevigata* is especially grown, cultivated, and appreciated in Japan. A few cultivars are available in the United States, and the list grows longer every year. The common name is quite appropriate, given the rounded, short, upright petals.

Iris laevigata requires moist soils throughout the entire year; it does not tolerate seasonal drought. It grows to about 36 inches (90 cm) tall with a spread of approximately 12 inches (30 cm). Because it prefers cooler summers, it usually reaches only 12–18 inches (30–45 cm) tall in our midwestern gardens. It is a much-favored plant in English water gardens and in Pacific Northwest ponds, but can be more difficult to establish in the southern and midwestern United States. Preferred water depth is from moist soil to 6 inches (15 cm) of water over the crown. Zones 4–9. Earned Royal Horticultural Society Award of Garden Merit in 1993.

The blossoms, usually 3–4 inches (7.5–10 cm) wide, are stunning additions to the pond garden. They appear in midsummer, sparkling white, elegant blue, or royal reddish purple blooms that dance over arching green foliage that sways in the breeze. The coloring is more like watercolors, not veined like the blooms of *Iris versicolor*.

Var. alba is a marvelous iris with snow white flowers having three drooping falls. It is often confused with 'Snowdrift', which has six falls.

'Albopurpurea' is taller with light blue flowers marked with a broad white border.

'Colchesterensis' is an older selection with six drooping falls. Its petals are pure white and heavily mottled in rich blue.

'Midnight Wine' was selected for its very deep maroon color. A slash of white marks the center of the falls.

'Monstrosa' has at least six falls, all medium blue edged in white, with a white signal spear washed with yellow.

'Mottled Beauty' is a full-flowering selection. The creamy white blooms are mottled with violet spots and streaks.

'Regal' is a lovely rose-magenta cultivar with flaring, slender falls.

'Royal Cartwheel' has blossoms of deep navy blue–purple, each petal carrying a slash of white down the center.

'Semperflorens' is another older cultivar, with deep blue-violet flowers. It frequently reblooms in the fall in the environment and climate it prefers.

'**Snowdrift**' has very clear, white blossoms marked with a yellow signal. It has six drooping falls and is often confused with *Iris laevigata* var. *alba*.

'**Variegata**' is cherished by water gardeners for its clean white stripes that run the length of each leaf. Blooms are a medium blue. Earned Royal Horticultural Society Award of Garden Merit in 1994.

'**Violet Parasol**' is a clear violet-blue, marked by a yellow spear in the center of each petal.

Iris versicolor
Blue flag, beet root iris

Iris versicolor produces light blue flowers in mid-spring. Native to North America, it is naturalized throughout eastern North America, from Canada southward to Texas and westward to the Mississippi Valley. Zones 3–9.

Iris versicolor grows to 24–30 inches (30–45 cm) tall and approximately 12 inches (30 cm) wide. It prefers water that is up to 3 inches (7.5 cm) or so over its crown. The flowers are 2 inches (5 cm) across and twice as abundant as those of *I. virginica*. Earned Royal Horticultural Society Award of Garden Merit in 1994.

'**Between the Lines**' is a free-flowering selection that reaches almost 24 inches (60 cm) high. The white flowers are heavily veined in violet, giving the blossoms a light blue appearance. A yellow signal on the falls adds a touch of a halo to the bloom.

'**Candystriper**' also grows to no more than 24 inches (60 cm). Its abundant white flowers are deeply veined in rose, giving them a pink glow.

'**Little Rhyme**' has clear white flowers with a bright yellow signal. It grows to about 12 inches (30 cm) high and blooms profusely. To date, this is by far the best white selection of *Iris versicolor*.

'**Mint Fresh**' is a slightly larger cultivar with bright white flowers that are heavily striped with red veining. The plentiful blossoms are reminiscent of peppermint candy.

'**Mysterious Monique**' is an extraordinary cultivar for the poolside garden. It flowers lib-

Iris laevigata 'Variegata'

Iris versicolor 'Mysterious Monique'

Iris virginica 'Dottie's Double'

erally, producing very dark violet petals, looking like black velvet, and accented by a distinct white signal. At almost 36 inches (90 cm) tall, it is eye-catching.

'**Party Line**' sports red-purple flowers veined in darker red-purple. It has a pale yellow signal that changes to white with red-purple veining. Style arms are pure white with a red-purple midrib. A most attractive and free-flowering cultivar, it grows to about 18 inches (45 cm) tall.

'**Pink Peaks**' is certainly the most diminutive cultivar available, growing to about 9 inches (23 cm) tall. A steady bloomer, it has dark pink flowers with red-purple veining. Its white signal is also veined in red-purple. Styles are dark pink with pure white curls on the tips.

'**Shape Up**' is distinctive for its orange-red signals veined in black and edged in white. Flowers are dark red-violet and are borne in profusion. This cultivar grows to about 18 inches (45 cm) tall.

Iris virginica
Blue flag, beet root iris

Iris virginica produces light blue flowers in midspring. Native to North America, it is naturalized from Canada southward to Texas and westward to the Mississippi Valley. Zones 4–9. Slightly taller than *I. versicolor*, it reaches up to 36 inches (90 cm) or more with a spread of about 12 inches (30 cm). It enjoys deeper water, up to 6 inches (15 cm) over its crown, and tolerates drought better than *I. versicolor*, making it a perfect plant for retention areas or wet spots in the lawn. The flowers are usually 2–4 inches (5–10 cm) wide.

'**Contraband Girl**' is bright blue with a hint of lavender. Sturdy and vigorous, it grows to about 36 inches (90 cm) tall.

'**Dottie's Double**' has unusual, double-petaled flowers veined in orchid-lavender. With six signals and six falls the flowers look like spinning pinwheels.

'**Pond Crown Point**' has large Cub Scout–blue flowers with strong yellow signals. It has good bud count on strong, erect stems.

'**Pond Lilac Dream**' has white flowers that unfurl to dainty lavender-pink, accented by a creamy yellow signal. It grows to about 4 feet (1.2 m) tall.

WATERLILY-LIKE PLANTS

Several very attractive plants grow like waterlilies but are not properly members of the genus *Nymphaea*. They produce rhizomes, tubers, and roots that grow in soil several inches, sometimes even several feet, below the water surface. With long stems or petioles, the plants bear foliage that floats on the water far above the soil surface. Their flowers also appear on, or above, the waterline. Apart from this common growth habit, waterlily-like plants are widely divergent in their plant shape and habit, flower color and size, and even their hardiness. Often waterlily-like plants are less expensive than waterlilies, and most of them grow and flower better in shade than do hardy or tropical waterlilies.

Landscape Uses

Waterlily-like plants are a great substitute for lilies in containers or in small ponds, especially in shady sites where lilies won't grow. Waterlily-like plants can also be used in regular ponds to force a perspective; to make a pond look wider and bigger, plant larger lilies in the front, dwarf lilies in the middle, and waterlily-like plants in the back. They add color and dimension along the edge of marginals or between rushes (*Scirpus*). Waterlily-like plants can add more color to a lotus or waterlily planting.

Optimal Growing Conditions

Sun: Full sun to shade.
Wind tolerance: Very little.
Water depth: Shallow, no more than 24 inches (60 cm).
Soil and water chemistry: Neutral to slightly acidic.
Temperature: Warm water 70°F (21°C) if plant is tender; cooler if plant is hardy.
Salt tolerance: None.

Seasonal Care

Spring: Fertilize hardy plants once they show active growth. Pot tender plants in fresh soil and fertilize them; return them to the pond once the water temperature consistently reaches 70°F (21°C).
Summer: Remove spent leaves and flowers. Fertilize plants regularly. When water temperature reaches 80°F (27°C), fertilize plants every two weeks.
Fall: Wind the runner back into the pot or simply cut it back to 12 inches (30 cm) or so from the base of the plant.
Winter: Submerge hardy plants to a depth in the pond where their rhizomes or crowns will not freeze. Bring tender plants indoors; keep them in an aquarium. Use a heater to maintain a water temperature of at least 70°F (21°) and lights to supply 12 hours of at least 1000 footcandles.

Planting

Waterlily-like plants are easy to pot up. Use wide, shallow pots and good aquatic soil, such as a clay and sand mix, or an equivalent. Soil-less media are acceptable but may be buoyant. Fill the pot with the soil, top with sand or pea gravel, and thoroughly water. Then make a hole in the soil, place the crown of the plant about 1 inch (2.5 cm) below the soil surface, and firm the soil over the roots. Submerge the pot in the pond, roughly 6 inches (15 cm) or so below the water surface. Because these plants have such brittle stems and dehydrate so easily, it is extremely important to keep them as moist as possible before they are transplanted, and to return them to the pond as soon as planting is done.

Opposite: Waterlily-like *Nymphoides geminata* is grown for its frilly, bright yellow flowers.

Aponogeton distachyus

Aponogeton distachyus
Water hawthorne

Aponogeton distachyus is one of more than 40 species in the genus *Aponogeton*, most of which have completely submerged foliage and flowers. It holds its blooms and leaves on the water surface and makes an extremely attractive plant in large ponds with cooler water. It flowers in spring and again in fall, and in warmer climates will often bloom all winter long. In colder areas, it can be grown indoors in the winter in a cool greenhouse or sun porch. Water hawthorne extends the season of flowers in the pond, blooming before waterlilies have begun to show color in the spring, and flowering again in the fall after waterlilies have ended their display. Native to South Africa, it has naturalized throughout Australia, New Zealand, and South America.

The flowers are a crisp white accented by black stamens, although variants can be found with lavender or even pink blooms. Flowers have a clean, vanilla fragrance that is carried on the wind for several feet. Foliage is elliptical, shiny, and dark green, sometimes with a tinge of purple. The plant grows in sun to part shade in water from 6 to 48 inches (15–120 cm) deep, spreading 24–30 inches (60–75 cm). It prefers cool water and may go completely dormant in ponds where the summer water temperature consistently exceeds 70°F (21°C). *Aponogeton distachyus* tolerates moving water. Although it can grow in deeper water, it performs best in 24 inches (60 cm) or less. The plant can withstand a freeze, needing no particular winter care or attention. Zones 5–11. It is also generally unaffected by pests or diseases.

Hydrocleys nymphoides
Water poppy

Hydrocleys nymphoides produces many floating runners, which quickly cover the water surface with leaves and blossoms. The plants are beneficial for their ability to provide this surface cover, but for this reason they may also be considered a nuisance in some areas and may be prohibited as a noxious weed in areas of the United States with warmer temperatures all year long.

The shiny, rounded leaves have a prominent midrib, and the creamy yellow flowers resemble single roses and are about 2 inches (5 cm) in diameter. An easy plant to grow, it starts blooming once the water temperature reaches 70–75°F (21–24°C) and continues unabated unless killed by frost. It is an excellent addition to ponds in cooler climates, where its running habit that spreads over 1–6 feet (30–180 cm) can be restrained. If the gardener is willing to prune it back, it grows well in container ponds and small water gardens.

Water poppy is also a favorite water plant because it tolerates a lot of shade, though it prefers sun, and grows in water as deep as 3 feet (90 cm), though it prefers 4–12 inches (10–30 cm). Because it is frost-tender, it must be brought indoors for the winter. Keep it in an aquarium with a grow light and a water heater. It may also be overwintered by keeping it moist in a hanging basket like a houseplant, although care must be

Hydrocleys nymphoides

taken lest it die due to the variation from its normal wet growing conditions. Zone (8)9.

Ludwigia sedioides
Mosaic plant

While most *Ludwigia* species are marginals that grow along the edge of the pond, *L. sedioides* grows as a mostly submerged plant. Its small, single yellow flowers bloom in summer. The diamond- to squarish-shaped leaves grow from a central radius so that the foliage forms a mosaic-like circle. The floating leaves are green with red edges, stems, and petioles. This unusual, attractive plant quickly provides water coverage in warm and sunny to partly shady conditions. It requires acidic or at least neutral water. Although it grows best in 12–18 inches (30–45 cm) of warm water, it survives depths of up to 36 inches (90 cm), as well as cooler water temperatures. Its running spread usually covers 24 inches (60 cm) in a single season, each rosette spreading to 4 inches (10 cm). The species is native to Brazil. Zones 8–11.

To overwinter the plant in cooler climates, bring it indoors and keep it in a warm aquarium of at least 65°F (18°C) with supplemental light to stretch the daylight the plant receives. In cool

Ludwigia sedioides

Nymphoides geminata

water or short days, it will produce dormant eyes or buds that fall to the bottom of the pond. Many gardeners have difficulty getting the buds to resprout in the spring. Other than the occasional aphid or China mark moth, the plant is not bothered by insects or diseases.

Nymphoides geminata
Yellow water snowflake

Nymphoides geminata is grown in larger ponds for its cheerful yellow, star-shaped flowers that have very frilly, fringed edges. Like water poppy (*Hydrocleys nymphoides*), it has floating stems that sprout, producing leaves, flowers, and still more rooted crowns. Both species have blooms that last only a day, but *N. geminata* has five petals per flower while *H. nymphoides* has only three. Leaves of the two species are rounded, but those of *N. geminata* have a sinus, are flatter and thinner, are often dark red or brown underneath, sometimes veined in burgundy on top, and have toothed or crinkled edges, while leaves of *H. nymphoides* have no sinus, are always green on both surfaces, and are always smooth-edged.

Nymphoides geminata is very free-flowering and fast growing, with a running spread, but can be controlled with pulling and spraying. In a pond, it seems to succumb to koi and goldfish so that it never gets out of hand, but never plant it in a natural body of water. It may be invasive. Ideally it grows in 4–24 inches (10–60 cm) of water, although it will grow in damp soil. It may be overwintered like hardy waterlilies, placed in the bottom of the pond where it will not freeze. Zones 5–11. Synonym *N. peltata*.

Nymphoides indica
White water snowflake

With frilly flowers similar to those of *Nymphoides geminata*, this white-flowered species is not as hardy. Furthermore, it sets blooms directly from the leaf axils rather than from running stems and thus does not have the overpowering coverage of other forms of the genus. It grows 12–24 inches (30–60 cm) or more wide in water 4–24 inches (10–60 cm) deep. The plant must be brought indoors in winter to be protected from cold tem-

Nymphoides indica

Polygonum amphibium

peratures. Keep it in an aquarium with a grow light and a small water heater. Zones 8–11.

'Gigantea' has flowers 1 inch (2.5 cm) or so wide and leaves up to 6 inches (15 cm) across. Its spread can be more than 36 inches (90 cm).

Polygonum amphibium
Willow grass, amphibious bistort

This lovely pond plant has long, narrow, floating leaves often tinged in red, accented by a red or black chevron and with a prominent midrib. In the summer, it produces hot pink flowers that resemble little bottle brushes. A versatile creeping plant, it adapts well to moist soil or as much as 4 feet (1.2 m) of water over its crown. When grown in the margin of the pond, it reaches up to 40 inches (100 cm) high. For optimal growth, place the plant in about 12–18 inches (30–45 cm) of water in sun to part shade. Zones 5–9.

FLOATING WATER PLANTS

Floating water plants are the ultimate in easy care water gardening—no potting is necessary. Like little boats, they simply drift effortlessly in the pond. Their roots dangle down into the water, drawing nutrients for the plant's growth. All floating water plants use their ability to float to exploit an environmental niche—growing in water that is too deep for other plants or that appears only seasonally, such as floodwater—to grow in water that is rich in nutrients.

Some of the best plants for filtering pond water are members of this group. They act as the pond's feather dusters, removing suspended particles from the water. Floating plants are important for shading the pond to protect fish and other wildlife from baking under the hot summer sun. The plants also provide a way for wildlife to hide from predators, such as herons and raccoons. Floating plants are fertile spawning grounds in the spring and hideaways for the young fry that hatch and grow in the summer.

The ease of care for which floating plants are so well known has also earned them considerable notoriety in warmer climates. In the United States, water hyacinth and water lettuce are not only discouraged but literally banned from possession in states from Florida to California. Never, never add a single floating plant to a natural body of water. Even in tiny portions, they can quickly grow and spread, causing enormous trouble with their floating mats of vegetation over the water. When in doubt, compost them into your vegetable bed.

Landscape Uses
Larger floating water plants, such as water lettuce (*Pistia stratiotes*) and water hyacinth (*Eich-*hornia crassipes*), grow well in ponds of all sizes. Keep them in the top, "header" pond of a stream or waterfall to aid in biological filtration. Smaller plants are more appropriate for container and tub gardens. In large, earthen ponds, it takes quite a few floaters to make an impression.

Too many floating plants covering a pond's surface can reduce oxygen in the water to levels that are dangerous to fish and other underwater animals. Complete cover is not a problem, however, in container water gardens that do not have any fish inhabitants. As a rule, about one-third of the pond's water surface should be covered with vegetation. As floating plants take over more of the pond in the late summer, they should be thinned and removed. Use them as mulch or compost, since they return nitrogen to the soil.

In ponds designed to house fish and other underwater wildlife, good choices are plants with long, flowing root systems, such as water hyacinth and water lettuce. These are favored by fish as ideal places to lay eggs during the spring spawning season. Aquatic insects and similar underwater inhabitants often use the long roots to hide and forage for still smaller aquatic wildlife that is a source of food.

For small container ponds on the deck or patio, or even in a window box, many of the floating plants make wonderful and easy-care accents. Smaller forms of water hyacinth and water lettuce, as well as water fern (*Ceratopteris thalictroides*), fit well into a mixed water planting of a container water feature.

Floating water plants absorb nitrates and phosphates from the water. Water hyacinth and water lettuce, in fact, are so efficient that they

Opposite: Tiny *Azolla* floats on the surface of a pond among a yellow-flowered hardy waterlily, *Nymphaea* 'Sioux', and upright, lance-leaved *Menyanthes*. Other water plants include *Acorus calamus* 'Variegatus' in front of a white rock, yellow-flowered *Nymphoides geminata* floating on the water surface to the right, dark-leaved *Colocasia esculenta* 'Black Magic' in the center background, and white-flowered *Hibiscus moscheutos* in the right background.

are often recommended to aid filtration. Their dangling roots quickly take in nutrients that would otherwise promote algae growth and turn the water green. Duckweeds (*Lemna*) are also able filtration plants, often used in sewage lagoons.

Optimal Growing Conditions

Sun: Full sun (even in harsh summer climates) to part shade.
Wind tolerance: Good.
Water depth: A few inches to several feet.
Soil and water chemistry: Acidic to alkaline.
Temperature: Warm water 65–80°F (18–27°C) and warm to hot, humid air even exceeding 100°F (35°C).
Salt tolerance: None.

Seasonal Care

Spring: Place hardy plants outdoors when pond temperature has reached a consistent 65°F (18°C). Move them to a shady spot in the pond when water temperature exceeds 80°F (27°C) and foliage starts to yellow. Tender plants thrive in heat and humidity, but their foliage turns yellow when the water temperature falls below 65°F (18°C).
Summer: Fertilize plants weekly by placing them in a separate bucket of pond water in which fertilizer has been dissolved at half the strength recommended by the manufacturer. Leave plants in the bucket overnight and then return them to the pond, rinsing the roots thoroughly so that the remnant fertilizer will not leach into the pond water and cause an algae bloom. Remove dead or tattered foliage and spent flowers as needed. Trim long, flowing roots back to 6–10 inches (15–25 cm) if they become too matted or dirty.
Winter: Bring tender plants indoors; keep them in an aquarium or float them in anything that can hold water, even a brandy snifter. Often they will do well in a warm sunny windowsill for several weeks, but then suddenly, in late winter, turn to mush and melt away. The problem is the lack of adequate light intensity. Tropical floating water plants need at least 14 hours of sunlight of at least 1000 foot-candles. This is equivalent to four fluorescent bulbs held about 12 inches (30 cm) over the water. Considering the amount of energy and electricity required to keep tropical water plants alive for an entire winter, it is often cheaper to simply mulch them into the vegetable garden in the fall and buy new plants the following spring.

Planting

Floating water plants are not usually grown in soil, but a few can be potted. This is often done in the winter to keep the plants growing indoors. Water hyacinth (*Eichhornia crassipes*) and water lettuce (*Pistia stratiotes*) may be grown in this fashion, although some gardeners prefer to grow them in pots so they stay contained and are easier to feed, leading to improved growth and better blooming. Once they are potted, however, they are unable to filter nutrients from the water and their value as filtration plants is essentially negated.

Azolla caroliniana
Fairy moss, mosquito fern

Native to North America, this species can be found growing wild as far north as Michigan and Wisconsin and into New England. Plants are rounded, not triangular, like branches of arborvitae (*Thuja*). They overwinter by freezing in the ice and thawing in spring.

A true fern, this aquatic has fuzzy, finely toothed leaves that are bright green in summer, and red in spring and fall when the water is cool. It makes an excellent pond cover for fish and other wildlife. It can withstand wind and wave movements even when completely upturned. Like other *Azolla* species, *A. caroliniana* holds a blue-green algae that fixes nitrogen, fertilizing the plants. It is very sensitive to the number of daylight hours it receives, giving it a tendency to die out during the shorter days of winter. It grows in sun to shade, reaching 1/2 inch (12 mm) high with a running spread. Zones 9–11. It can be overwintered on moist soil or a similar growing medium.

Azolla caroliniana in cool water

Ceratopteris thalictroides
Water fern

This unusual floating plant is said to resemble a fern because of its highly cut and serrated leaves, which look like the big, puffy leaves of Italian parsley. The plant usually reaches 12 inches (30 cm) high and wide. Any part of the foliage that lies on the water surface sprouts a plantlet and will root to become a new plant. Water fern also grows in soil in a few inches of water; when so planted, its foliage looks like curly parsley, still more finely cut. It grows best in full shade and needs at least part shade to survive. To overwinter water fern, keep it in water of at least 65°F (18°C). Bring it indoors into a warm fish tank. It is not bothered by pests or diseases. Zones 9–11.

Ceratopteris thalictroides

Eichhornia crassipes

Eichhornia crassipes
Water hyacinth

Noted for its prominent lavender-blue flowers and fleshy, shiny green, rounded, floating leaves, *Eichhornia crassipes* grows quickly in warm water, reaching about 12 inches (30 cm) high with a running spread. Leaves are spongy and inflated at the base, making them buoyant in water. A few plants bought in the spring can easily turn into a few hundred by fall (they are excellent for compost in the perennial border or the vegetable garden). The species is prohibited in the southern United States because of its ability to clog waterways. Where it can be grown legally, it is a welcome addition to the water garden for its ability to filter out unwanted nutrients and for its attractive flowers. Although each flower lasts only a day or two, the flowers are borne in abundance. The species is believed to be native to Africa. Zones 9–11.

Eichhornia crassipes grows best in sun to part shade in warm water and will not survive a winter freeze. Because cool spring temperatures can cause severe setback, wait until the pond temperature is consistently at 65°F (18°C) before putting plants out in the spring. In colder climates, treating them like annuals is easiest and often cheapest. Overwintering them requires water temperatures of at least 60°F (16°C) and sunlight for at least 10 hours every day.

Eichhornia crassipes is so highly regarded for its filtration abilities—its roots draw nutrients out of the water—that it is routinely grown for sewage treatment. It also absorbs pollutants such as heavy metals. Like other tender floating aquatic species of *Eichhornia*, it makes a great container plant. In larger bodies of water it can even grow into a large mat that will absorb some of the motion associated with waves or wind.

LEMNA
Duckweed

Known as the smallest flowering plants in the world, duckweeds typically have leaves that are round or almost round. These are light green and less than 1/8 inch (4 mm) in diameter, with a single root growing from the underside of the

Lemna

leaf. Although the plants do flower, the minute blooms defy detection by the naked eye. Zones 3–11.

Duckweeds grow in sun to part shade with a running spread, quickly covering the water surface. They have "budding pouches" on the edge of the leaf, from which grow new single-leafed plants. Plants overwinter by producing buds that sink to the bottom of the pond.

Duckweed is often seen covering large areas of earthen ponds. It can withstand wind and wave movements even when completely upturned. Fish love to eat it. It can be planted as a food source for koi and goldfish to eat in early spring when it is still too early to feed them regular fish food. Adding goldfish to a pond is an excellent way to rid the water of duckweed in a short time, without having to resort to the use of harmful pesticides.

Pistia stratiotes
Water lettuce

The foliage grows like a rosette from a single crown and really does resemble a floating head of lettuce or cabbage. The leaves, which are spongy, crinkled, velvety, and usually light green to lime green, have water-repellent hairs that use surface tension to allow the leaf literally to stand on the water. When mature, each leaf may reach up to 12 inches (30 cm) high and several inches

Pistia stratiotes

Pistia stratiotes 'Angyo Splash'

wide. An individual plant overall may reach more than 24 inches (60 cm) in diameter, though water lettuce has a running spread. This species grows best in part shade, especially in very hot climates, and can tolerate full shade. Flowers are tiny, white circles that appear just at the base of the leaves. Something akin to microscopic peace lilies, they are only visible by searching for them. Water lettuce reproduces by offsets that grow from the base of the mature plant, like strawberry plants. It is difficult to overwinter. A plant can grow into a large mat that will absorb some of the motion associated with waves or wind. Zones 9–11.

'**Angyo Splash**' (variegated water lettuce) is a Japanese selection with leaves streaked and blotched in creamy yellow. Like many variegated plants, it has a tendency to revert.

'**Aqua Velvet**' (blue water lettuce) has light blue flowers and is only about 6 inches (15 cm) high and wide, making it more suitable than the species for smaller backyard ponds.

'**Ruffles**' (ruffled water lettuce), only 2–4 inches (5–10 cm) tall and wide, has leaves with top edges more crinkled and ruffled than the species.

SUBMERGED WATER PLANTS

Submerged water plants help filter unwanted nutrients and add important oxygen to the water during the day. Many are highly decorative as well. Some grow well in moving water, such as the pockets in streams and under waterfalls. Others require still, placid water to grow well. Certain submerged plants were once popular in aquariums, but having become troublesome weeds in natural lakes and streams may be unlawful to sell or keep under applicable laws. Fortunately, alternatives to those prohibited plants are available that are helpful to the pond ecology.

Underwater plants are sometimes referred to as oxygenators because they add oxygen to the water in the pond. This label is a bit of a misnomer, since submerged plants produce oxygen only during the day. At night, they reverse the process and remove oxygen from the water. Many marginal pond plants have submerged forms often sold as oxygenators, although they do not perform in the pond as they do in the fish tank.

Plant Parts and Habit

Submerged plants with floating flowers often bloom in late spring or early summer, sometimes continuing intermittently throughout the summer. Although each blossom may be very small, a large grouping can make an attractive addition to the early summer pond, when waterlilies have only just begun to flower, or to accompany water hawthorne (*Aponogeton distachyus*).

Foliage of submerged water plants is very distinct from that of emerged plants. Some leaves are thick and straplike, while others are very thin and finely cut. Often the leaves and stems are easily torn or broken; since they are viviparous, this brittleness permits the plants' proliferation in a wide area, especially in large earthen ponds, where they can quickly overrun the bottom of the pond.

Roots of underwater plants are often long and fibrous, serving both to anchor the plant and to draw nutrients from the soil. The exception is hornworts, which have no roots to speak of but instead float in the water and absorb nutrients through their foliage. Many underwater plants that root in the soil produce subsoil runners from which new plantlets quickly sprout. These plants are able to form a carpet on the pond floor that holds soil in place, much like a sod.

Landscape Uses

Thanks to their diversity, submerged plants can be selected to grow well in almost any kind of pond or water garden setting. *Ranunculus* flourishes in calm or moving water. Dwarf forms of hornwort thrive in just a few inches of water in a table-top pond.

In a pond for fish and wildlife, most oxygenators make good spawning beds but are hard to remove from the pond when the fish are done. *Utricularia* species, though, do not seek to root, making them excellent spawning grounds for fish in the spring. You can dip out the plant and move it to a new home to raise the fry if you like. Also, because of the course texture of the plants, the fish tend not to eat them.

Submerged plants perform a vital role in creating and maintaining an ecosystem suitable for fish and other wildlife. Through photosynthesis, these plants draw nutrients directly from the water, absorbing nitrates and phosphates through their leaves as well as their roots. Submerged plants also make great dust mops. As they photosynthesize, their leaves become charged and attract dust and dirt out of the water column, effectively cleaning the water. Too much dirt in the water can eventually kill the plants by interfering with photosynthesis, but too many submerged plants in a small pond can cause violent pH swings from day to night because of their oxygenating properties. Most lined ornamental ponds benefit from 10 to 15 bunches of oxygenators for every 200–300 cubic feet (6–8-1/2 m^3) of water.

Ranunculus aquatilis grows submerged and can send up emergent leaves and flowers.

Optimal Growing Conditions

Sun: Full sun to shade, depending on the species or cultivar.

Wind tolerance: None to good, depending on the species or cultivar.

Water depth: 4–72 inches (10–180 cm) deep in clear water.

Soil and water chemistry: Acidic to neutral.

Temperature: Warm water no more than 90°F (32°C).

Salt tolerance: None.

Seasonal Care

Summer: Fertilize regularly according to the manufacturer's directions. Remove old, tattered leaves. Trim long stems as needed for appearance. Plants that grow from underground stolons often need no additional care except an occasional brushing of their leaves to remove accumulated soil, algae, or similar debris.

Fall: Stop fertilizing submerged plants about three weeks before the average frost date. In frost-free climates, stop fertilizing when the pond temperature falls below 60°F (16°C).

Winter: Leave submerged plants in the pond. Bring tender plants indoors; submerge them in a bowl of water or fish tank, and set them on a warm, sunny windowsill.

Planting

Submerged plants grow best if they are planted in a pot and fertilized regularly. Use a wide, shallow pot (a cat-litter tray works well), or plant them in the same pot with waterlilies or water hawthorne (*Aponogeton distachyus*). Use clay mixed with sand, or an equivalent. Gravel is also acceptable, although it will not hold fertilizer.

All stem-cut submerged plants are planted in a similar way. First, fill the pot with soil and top off with sand or pea gravel. Water the soil thoroughly. Put a hole in the center of the pot about 2 inches (5 cm) deep, and insert 5 to 10 stems. Push the soil back around the stems and submerge the pot in the pond. Some under-

water plants may also be grown in a pond by gently tying them to a rock at the bottom of the pond.

For plants that grow from a main crown, fill a pot slightly more than half full of soil. Set the plant on top of the soil and spread the roots over the soil surface. Cover the roots with sand, taking care not to cover the crown of the plant. If fish dig through the sand, top it with some gravel.

Submerged plants are often sold as unpotted bunched stems or clumps. Lead weights are sometimes attached so that the plants may be simply sunk to the bottom of the pond. If you purchase a bunch that has been sold with a lead weight, simply remove the weight before pushing the stems into the soil.

Elodea canadensis

Often mistaken for the dreaded *Hydrilla verticillata*, a very pernicious water weed that is illegal to grow, sell, or transport anywhere in the United States, *Elodea canadensis* is easily distinguished by having only three leaves at each segment, while *H. verticillata* has five leaves per segment. Because *E. canadensis* does well in cool pond temperatures, it is widely available in England. The plant produces female flowers with three small white petals that float on the water surface. The flowers bloom in late summer or whenever the stems reach the surface. Male flowers are rarely produced because male plants are rare. Flowers are seldom fertile, so the plant usually spreads by fragments rather than seed production.

Elodea canadensis is great for the native pond in the United States and Canada, with a few native fish, like sunfish or blue gills, that do not eat plants. It is also suitable for smaller ponds that do not have fish, which like to graze on its foliage and can easily break its brittle stems. It does poorly in moving water, where the plants tends to break up and uproot.

Elodea canadensis grows well in fairly cool water that is on the alkaline side. It does best in

Elodea canadensis

fine sand with a small amount of organic matter. It grows in full sun or shade, but becomes much more stringy in shade. It spreads 12 inches (30 cm) and reaches 2 inches to 6 feet (5–180 cm) tall from the base of the plant. Water depth can be as little as 6 inches (15 cm) or as much as 40 feet (12 m), as long as it is clear. *Elodea canadensis* overwinters as an evergreen and continues to photosynthesize even under ice, albeit at a reduced rate. Zones 3–9.

Ranunculus longirostris
White water buttercup, white water crowfoot

The genus *Ranunculus* includes more than 400 species, about three dozen of which grow in aquatic conditions. Found throughout all temperate and tropical regions of the world, a few are often sold for their underwater ornamental value. These grow well in sun to part shade in water 1–6 feet (30–180 cm) deep. They spread about 1 foot (30 cm) wide, with stems reaching 6–48 inches (15–120 cm) or more in length. They flower on the water's surface in late spring or early summer. They overwinter easily below the freeze line. Koi destroy them, however. *Ranunculus* species do well in slowly to moderately moving water and look great in pond narrows. Zones 4–11.

Ranunculus longirostris has leaves that are very finely cut, open, and airy, almost thread-like. They are borne alternately, radiating from a central stem. The plant starts growing in early spring and prefers cool water. The flowers float on the water surface. Stems are brittle and break easily when handled. The plant grows quickly from leaf nodes and branches very readily. In still or slow-moving water, it can form dense stands. This North American native is very ornamental and should find a home in all ponds. It is not invasive. Large stands of it are very beautiful in flower, looking like snow on the water.

Ranunculus longirostris, submerged form

Ranunculus longirostris, terrestrial form

UTRICULARIA
Bladderwort

A member of a carnivorous family, the genus Utricularia comprises about 260 species, found naturalized in most of the temperate and tropical climates of the world. Many species are native to North America and provide food and cover for fish. Bladderworts make unusual submerged plants for the pond or the aquarium. Some have very fine foliage. Others look almost like floating green bits of hairnet or string algae. Nestled among the foliage are the tiny "bladders" that trap prey, microscopic creatures that are unwary enough to trigger the bladders' openings only to get sucked in and digested.

The foliage grows as floating mats underwater and in some species can reach several feet in length and spread. Each stem is usually 2–24 inches (5–60 cm) or more long and 1–6 inches (2.5–15 cm) wide. The late-summer flowers are yellow, white, pink, or purple. The dainty blossoms stand above the water surface and resemble small snapdragons. Submerged bladderworts do not produce roots, so no soil or potting is necessary. These are fascinating and great plants for kids.

Bladderworts do not tolerate new ponds, but three- or four-year-old ponds should be suitable. Most bladderworts prefer neutral to acidic

Utricularia

water in full sun to part shade. Plants float just below the surface, so the water has to be just deep enough to keep them covered. Zones 3–11. To overwinter plants, allow the buds that form just before winter to sink below the freeze line, or bring plants or buds indoors into a fish tank.

The best species to grow submerged are **Utricularia floridana**, which is quite large and showy; **U. inflata**; **U. minor**, which is very easy; **U. radiata**; and **U. vulgaris**, which is very large, like hornwort. All these have yellow flowers. A purple-flowered option is **U. purpurea**.

USDA HARDINESS ZONE MAP

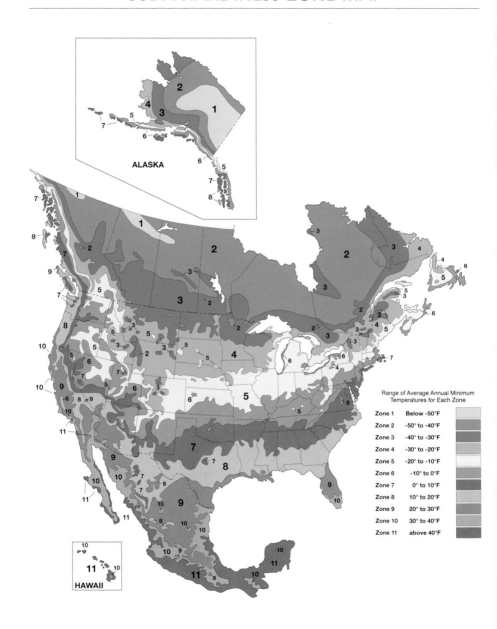

Range of Average Annual Minimum
Temperatures for Each Zone

Zone 1	Below -50°F
Zone 2	-50° to -40°F
Zone 3	-40° to -30°F
Zone 4	-30° to -20°F
Zone 5	-20° to -10°F
Zone 6	-10° to 0°F
Zone 7	0° to 10°F
Zone 8	10° to 20°F
Zone 9	20° to 30°F
Zone 10	30° to 40°F
Zone 11	above 40°F

ALASKA

HAWAII

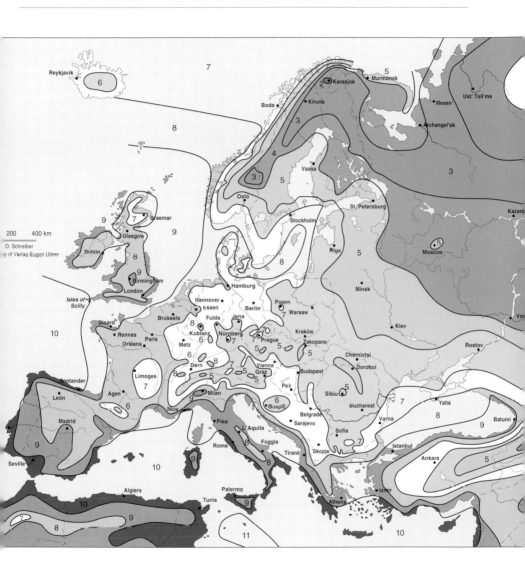

NURSERY SOURCES

This is a partial list of nurseries that specialize in aquatic plants. No endorsement is intended, nor is criticism implied of sources not mentioned. Most good local garden centers usually stock water garden plants.

Canada
Burns Water Gardens
2419 Van Luven Road
Baltimore, Ontario
Canada
(905) 372-2737
www.burnswatergardens.ca

United Kingdom
Bennetts Water Gardens
Putton Lane
Chickerell, Weymouth
Dorset DT3 4AF England
01305 785150
www.waterlily.co.uk

Bodmin Plant and Herb Nursery
Laveddon Mill
Bodmin
Cornwall PL30 5JU England
01208 72837
www.bodminnursery.co.uk

Dorset Water Lily Company
Yeovil Road
Halstock, Yeovil
Somerset BA22 9SB England
01935 891668
www.dorsetwaterlily.co.uk

Merebrook Pond Plants
Merbrook Farm
Hanley Swan
Worcestershire WR8 0DX England
01684 310950
www.pondplants.co.uk

Mickfield Watergarden Centre
Mickfield
Debenham
Suffolk IP14 5LP England
01449 711336
www.watergardenshop.co.uk

Paul Bromfield Aquatics
Gosmore
Hitchin
Hertfordshire SG4 7QD UK England
01462 457399
www.bromfieldaquatics.co.uk

Penlan Perennials
Penrhiw-pal
Llandysul
Ceredigion SA44 5QH Wales
01239 851244
www.penlanperennials.co.uk

Rowden Gardens
Brentor
Tavistock
Devon PL19 0NG England
01822 810275
www.rowdengardens.com

Rumsey Gardens
117 Drift Road
Clanfield, Waterlooville
Hants PO8 0PD England
02392 593367
www.rumsey-gardens.co.uk

Stapeley Water Gardens
London Road
Natwich
Cheshire CW5 7LH England
01270 623868
www.stapeleywg.com

The Water Garden
Hinton Parva
Swindon
Wiltshire SN4 0DH England
01793 790558
www.thewatergarden.co.uk

Water Meadow Nursery
Water Meadows
Cheriton, near Alresford
Hampshire SO24 0QB England
01962 771895
www.plantaholic.co.uk

United States
Bergen Water Gardens and Nursery
7443 Buffalo Road
Churchville, New York 14428
(585) 293-2860
www.bergenwatergardens.com

Green and Hagstrom Aquatic Nursery
7767 Fernvale Road
Fairview, Tennessee 37062
(615) 799-0708
www.greenandhagstrom.com

Hughes Water Gardens
25289 SW Stafford Road
Tualatin, Oregon 97062
(503) 638-1709
www.hugheswatergardens.com

Lilypons Water Gardens
6800 Lily Pon Road
Adamstown, Maryland 21710
(800) 999-5459
www.lilypons.com

Maryland Aquatic Nurseries
3427 North Furnace Road
Jarrettsville, Maryland 21084
(410) 557-7615
www.marylandaquatic.com

Nelson Water Gardens
1502 Katy Fort Bend County Road
Katy, Texas 77493
(281) 391-4769
www.nelsonwatergardens.com

Oasis Water Gardens
404 South Brandon Street
Seattle, Washington 98101
(206) 767-9776
www.oasiswatergardens.com

Perry's Water Gardens
136 Gibson Aquatic Farm Road
Franklin, North Carolina 28734
(828) 524-3264
www.perryswatergardens.net

Plant Delights Nursery
9241 Sauls Road
Raleigh, North Carolina 27603
(919) 772-4794
www.plantdelights.com

Ponds of Reflection
26425 Leeward Street
Eustis, Florida 32736
(352) 357-6200
www.pondsofreflection.com

Star Ridge Aquatics
180 Star Ridge Road
Carthage, North Carolina 28327
(910) 947-5333
www.starridgeaquatics.com

Tropical Pond and Garden
17928 61st Place North
Loxahatchee, Florida 33470
(561) 791-8994
www.tropicalpond.com

Van Ness Water Gardens
2460 North Euclid Avenue
Upland, California 91784
(877) 987-5459
www.vnwg.com

Yucca Do Nursery
P.O. Box 907
Hempstead, Texas 77445
(979) 826-4580
www.yuccado.com

GLOSSARY

Bract A modified leaf; a leaflike structure

Catkin A stalkless flower, as seen in all cattails (*Typha*)

Changeable waterlily A waterlily with flowers that open in one shade of color and then mature or fade to another

Circumboreal Distributed or occurring chiefly throughout the northern temperate zone

Coin leaves The small, new leaves on a lotus before they mature into floating leaves

Corm The swollen base of a stem, as seen in water plantain (*Alisma*)

Cosmopolitan Distributed almost anywhere around the world, as is true of water primrose (*Ludwigia*)

Crown The base of a plant

Deadhead To pull dead or dying flowers off a plant

Falls The drooping outer petals of an *Iris* flower

Hardy waterlily A waterlily that will survive a cold winter and thus can be left outdoors year-round

Indicator leaves Thin, transparent leaves on hardy waterlilies that tell the plant when it should start growing in the spring or stop growing in the fall

Petiole Leaf stalk

Revert To return to its original state, as when an all-green leaf appears on a plant that usually bears variegated leaves

Rhizome An underground horizontal stem, as seen in *Iris* species

Rosette A formation of leaves radiating from a crown, as seen in water lettuce (*Pistia stratiotes*)

Senesence The process of dying off

Signal In *Iris* flowers, a patch of color surrounding or forming a flare on the falls

Sinus The space between the lobes of a waterlily

Spathe A leaf or bract that encloses a flower

Standards The upper petals of an *Iris* flower

Stolon An aboveground horizontal stem

Tropical waterlily A waterlily that cannot grow outdoors year-round; tender

Tuber The underground storage organ of certain plants

Turion A small growth on an underground tuber, which sprouts and develops into a new plant. Common in arrowheads (*Sagittaria*)

Umbel A flower head in which the individual flower stems arise from a common point, as in water lettuce (*Pistia stratiotes*)

Viviparous Able to produce new plants while still attached to the parent plant

FURTHER READING

Chatto, Beth. 2005. *Beth Chatto's Damp Garden: Moisture-Loving Plants for Year-Round Interest*. London: Orion Publishing Group.

McEwen, Currier. 1990. *The Japanese Iris*. Hanover, Massachusetts: Brandeis University Press.

Rice, Barry A. 2006. *Growing Carnivorous Plants*. Portland, Oregon: Timber Press.

Slocum, Perry. 2005. *Water Lilies and Lotuses: Species, Cultivars, and New Hybrids*. Portland, Oregon: Timber Press.

Society for the Louisiana Iris. 2000. *The Louisiana Iris: The Taming of a Native American Wildflower*. 2nd ed. Portland, Oregon: Timber Press.

Speichert, Greg, and Sue Speichert. 2004. *Encyclopedia of Water Garden Plants*. Portland, Oregon: Timber Press.

Swindells, Philip. 2000. *Popular Pond Plants*. Dorking, Surrey, United Kingdom: Interpet Publishing.

Watanabe, Satomi. 1990. *The Fascinating World of Lotus*. Japan.

INDEX